To Dr. Thomas Sowell,
preeminent and courageous social scientist,
and intellectual inspiration to me for forty years

CONTENTS

PREFACE

While I am constrained to write this book, I realize that any such effort is faced with multiple challenges. It is a weighty task, and risky. First, given the welter of often-conflicting accounts on our cultural and political situation, finding reliable sources is not simple. I hope to avoid unreliable sources and root my analysis in credible ones. Second, one needs to develop a biblical view of race and justice to bring to bear on our vexed situation. Third is the need to understand Critical Race Theory (CRT) in its several forms aright. Fourth, one must have an accurate understanding of the history of race and gender in America—no small task. Finally, some advice—I won't say a *solution*—should be given that is biblical, hopeful, and realistic.

In attempting these four tasks, I hope to avoid mere talking points, factoids, clichés, and ideological shibboleths. Nevertheless, my political views will emerge in the chapters that follow. I will argue for them while anticipating criticisms and will advance credible viewpoints whether these are acceptable to those on the right, the left, or the middle politically. My theological commitments are to historic Christian orthodoxy. My social and political views are largely informed by the tradition of classical liberalism, which is not to be confused with contemporary liberalism or leftism.[1] This view is often called *conservative*, but I mean that not in the sense of being a Republican (I am unaffiliated with any political party), but of sharing in the vision of people like the Irish statesman Edmund Burke (1729–1797) and more recent American thinkers such as Russell Kirk (1918–1994) and Thomas Sowell (b. 1930).

A conservative in my sense holds what Sowell calls a "constrained vision" of human nature, institutions, and history.[2] This account takes humans to be constitutionally limited in their knowledge and goodness. Therefore, social and political aims should be calibrated accordingly in order to avoid utopian ends which are both unachievable and (ironically) deleterious to society. This means that statecraft is concerned with establishing and preserving order, policing the law, conserving historic institutions (such as the nuclear family and the church), and ensuring legal equality for all persons as a fundamental right.

Unlike the "unconstrained vision," this account denies that any revolution or social program will bring about a society unaffected by humankind's basic selfishness and other intrinsic limitations. A conservative is skeptical of any plans to *eliminate* poverty, racism, sexism, or any other ills, since humanity is not subject to such perfections. We will find that just as the American war on poverty inadvertently made many matters worse, thus injuring the ones it sought to save, so too do today's efforts to eliminate racism and other social ills.

A conservative seeks to ameliorate ills as much as possible and is quick to critique ill-fated and unrealistic attempts to fundamentally change human nature. Conservatives, given their constrained view, are eagle-eyed to spot the unintended consequences of political overreach (or statism). We will find that well-meaning measures, such as minimum-wage laws, preferential admission policies based on race, taxing the rich at a higher rate than others, and affirmative action, end up doing more harm than good. The policies proposed by "antiracism" are even more draconian and dangerous, despite the colorful name. As the adage puts it, "The best laid plans of mice and men often go awry."

Radical-turned-conservative David Horowitz explains another crucial aspect of the conservative vision.

> Conservative principles are about limits, and what the respect for limits makes possible. By contrast, progressive views [of which CRT is one] are built on expectations about the future. Progressive principles are based on ideas about a world that does not exist. For progressives, the future is not a maze of human uncertainties and unintended consequences, but a moral choice. To achieve "social justice" requires only that enough people will it.[3]

Thus, all progressives, and especially CRT advocates, focus more on denigrating the status quo as racist, sexist, homophobic, classist, etc., than on preserving legitimate institutions or explicating just how the desired "social justice" should play out. Idealism is unshaped by realism and often results in de facto nihilism—the system must be destroyed and we will worry about how to rebuild it later (if at all). As Black Lives Matter leader Hawk Newsome put it,

> If this country doesn't give us what we want, then we will burn down this system and replace it. All right? And I could be speaking figuratively. I could be speaking literally. It's a matter of interpretation.[4]

Given the riots of the summer of 2020, we know what the proper interpretation was.

This constrained vision is founded on a Judeo-Christian world-view anthropology. Humans, while made in the Divine Image, are fallen and sinful (Genesis 1–3; Romans 3:9–20). We are unique and uniquely valuable among the living, but are likewise prone to selfishness, self-deception, and cruelty. The ultimate remedy for this sad condition is divine deliverance found in Jesus Christ as Savior and Lord. Still, those delivered from the penalty of sin through faith in the Mediator do not become angels upon their conversion, and many never convert. Thus, any social and political policy should heed intrinsic human failings, turpitude, and outright evil. Otherwise, such a policy or movement will try to draw blood from a turnip and will shed innocent blood along the way.

So, let us begin. I ask only of my reader that he or she read carefully, check the documentation, and endeavor to serve God and others even as there is fire in the streets and fire in the minds of men and women.[5]

WHO STARTED THE FIRE?

We saw fire in the streets across America in the hot, pandemic summer of 2020. Some were horrified and some were gratified. It all started after a short video was leaked to the press that showed a black man dying on May 25, 2020, while a white police officer had him pinned to the ground with his knee. That man was crying out, "I can't breathe!" That phrase became a rallying cry for those who saw the death of forty-six-year-old George Floyd as emblematic of racism in America. On this basis—and before a trial was held—hundreds of protests turned into riots across America.[1] Not all were violent, but thousands of police were accosted, highways were blocked, businesses were looted, and federal and other buildings were set ablaze.

According to the Center for Disaster Philanthropy, "[b]etween May 25 and November 18, 2020, protests occurred in more than 4,446 cities worldwide, including in all states, territories and Washington, D.C., and internationally in more than 60 countries."[2] Nineteen people were killed during the first two weeks of protests. Americans, especially those in inner cities, were on high alert all summer.[3] Sales of guns skyrocketed, breaking records.[4] Amid all this, we heard calls to "defund the police," that America was "systemically racist," and that white people experience an unjust "white privilege."

For many, the death of George Floyd sparked a national "reckoning on race." Some take it as the beginning of a positive revolution. Others fear it may mean the end of America as we know it. When added to concerns about the deaths of other black people—such as Trayvon Martin and Breonna Taylor—at the hands of white police officers,[5] Floyd's dramatic and globally publicized death was the tipping point that drove people into the streets, often to commit violence. Floyd's image was seen everywhere—on posters, on murals, on shirts, and on street signs. While millions were mandated to stay inside because of the pandemic, multitudes were allowed to protest freely without masks and without censure.

Some even justified the extensive looting of 2020 riots by saying that the rioters and looters, who were people of color (POC), deserved the goods, since the owners' insurance would replace the goods and pay for the damage. Vicky Osterweil, author of *In Defense of Looting*,[6] told National Public Radio (which is supported by tax dollars) that

> when I use the word looting, I mean the mass expropriation
> of property, mass shoplifting during a moment of upheaval
> or riot. That's the thing I'm defending.

She wants revenge on those who have supposedly succeeded at the expense of black people.[7]

Will such attacks make white people fairer and more generous with black people? Will these attacks bring down the whole system of private property in the United States? They will not, unless millions start wantonly breaking the law by looting. Moreover, property is not based on white supremacy but is a natural right of all citizens. Why strike "at the heart...of the police?"[8] Many police officers—including police chiefs—are black. At their best, they try to keep the peace and protect the innocent. To deny the institution of policing is to live in a dangerous fantasy world wherein people will just get along if freed from police, given enough welfare and social workers. Osterweil's proposal is sheer *ressentiment*—and is, as such, ugly as sin, because sin it is. "You shall not steal" (Exodus 20:15), God declared.

In the days before the verdict on Derek Chauvin—the white officer whose knee was on George Floyd—businesses were boarded up in cities across the country, including Denver, Colorado, where I live. Because Chauvin was convicted of second-degree unintentional murder, third-degree murder, and second-degree manslaughter, few protests followed. America had not seen this kind of upheaval since the riots of 1968, and many wondered how it would end.

This fire in the streets stemmed from the fire in the minds of many about race, class, and gender. This fire is strange fire, not holy fire. While many are rightly concerned about racial justice, economic opportunity, and the fair treatment of LGBTQ people, the leading philosophy behind these protests is CRT. This philosophy that has driven people to torch the streets is being taught in state schools and has been implemented in the military and in governmental settings. Christopher F. Rufo, a senior fellow at the Manhattan Institute, wrote that

> [i]n Cupertino, California, an elementary school forced first-graders to deconstruct their racial and sexual identities, and rank themselves according to their "power and privilege." ... The Treasury Department held a training session telling staff members that "virtually all white people contribute to racism" and that they must convert

"everyone in the federal government" to the ideology
of "antiracism."[9]

I will give many more examples in the pages to come, but behind
these events lies the basic theory of CRT.

What Is Critical Race Theory?

In a nutshell, CRT developed from an earlier ideology called
Critical Theory (CT), which was a form of neo-Marxism. Every
aspect of society must be criticized and found wanting. Instead of
dividing society into the two categories of the bourgeoise owners (the
oppressors) and the proletariat workers (the oppressed), as in
Marxism, CT taught that oppression is woven into the fabric of culture and must be exposed through cultural critique. Through this
critique, the culturally and economically oppressed can throw off their
"false consciousness" (socially induced deceptions about their plight)
and embrace a philosophy of liberation.

CT morphed into CRT when legal scholars began to add race to
the mix, seeing racism as systemic in American life and evident in the
law. Thinkers like the late Derrick Bell, best known for his work with
the National Association for the Advancement of Colored People,
argue that white racism has been a permanent feature of American
life and could only be countered by revolutionary change in cultural
and political values. Those advancing rights for sexual minorities
(lesbians, gays, bisexuals, the transgendered, etc.) found the social
system to be rigged against them as well. For that reason, I will include
gender matters under CRT in upcoming chapters.[10] Today, this amal-
gamation plays out in the following ideas, advanced by thinkers such
as Kimberlé Crenshaw, Robin DiAngelo, and Ibram X. Kendi.

CRT claims that America is systemically racist and that the entire
social system disadvantages POC—a term which includes all

non-white people, but which usually refers to African Americans. Any discrepancy in the achievements between POC and white people is due primarily, or entirely, to this systemic racism. The claim of systemic racism is often accompanied by the idea that America has been racist from its beginning. The 1619 Project, a long-form journalism project of the *New York Times* that aims to reframe national history, claims that America was founded on racism when the first slaves were brought here in 1619. Any idea of "American exceptionalism" is therefore deemed racist, xenophobic, and so on.

All white people are racist, say CRT advocates. They grant that not all white people harbor explicit ill will toward POC, but since they are part of a racist system, they participate in racism simply by being white. They must be taught to realize this, which is the goal of the popular book *White Fragility* by Robin DiAngelo. White people, particularly heterosexual white males, are the oppressors in society. Let us consider some terms and phrases used in CRT.

"White privilege" refers to the condition of unearned and unjust benefits—economic, cultural, and emotional—that POC and sexual minorities do not experience.

"White supremacy" is the ideology that says white people will fight to keep their white privilege over POC, even if they do so unconsciously. This is a redefinition of the classic sense of the term, which held that white supremacy is "the belief that the white race is inherently superior to other races and that white people should have control over people of other races."[11]

"Racial essentialism" is a tricky term. On the one hand, CRT says that race is "constructed" socially and not inherent in people. In this sense, it is postmodern.[12] On the other hand, race is what determines whether one is oppressed or an oppressor. How this conflict is resolved escapes me, but perhaps it can be claimed that racial conceptions are constructed by the oppressors in order to oppress. As such, they are real. But in terms of one's objective being, they are false.

"Standpoint epistemology" is the belief that, unlike white people, POC and sexual minorities have a privileged perspective on matters of racial oppression. Their "lived experience" defines objective reality. If someone questions that perspective, he or she is assumed to be racist. Thus, CNN host Don Lemon often speaks of "his truth" of experiencing racism and homophobia as a gay black man, as do others seeking to advance this agenda.

"Intersectionality" is an idea Kimberlé Crenshaw developed, holding that those who occupy several oppressed categories—such as a black lesbian or a Hispanic transgender person—are particularly oppressed, and thus have a reliable vantage point to speak of the dynamics of oppression.[13]

"Identity politics" is the norm amongst advocates of CRT. Instead of deeming individuals as "created equal" before God and the law, CRT understands individuals as members of a group who must be treated accordingly. Hence, the proliferation of hyphenated adjectives: African-Americans, Hispanic-Americans, and more.

"Microaggressions" are commonly perceived by CRT enthusiasts. Given the above points, white people often disrespect and disadvantage POC through subtly abusive figures of speech and gestures. Given standpoint epistemology, a microaggression identified by a POC or sexual minority cannot be questioned.

Free speech is not typically valued in CRT. Because of the points above, some speech is deemed as tainted at the source and, as such, does not have the right to be heard. This is evidenced by the numerous public officials and private citizens who have been deplatformed at public events or banned from social media. CRT deems the older American notion of an open "marketplace of ideas" to be a prop for white privilege.[14]

As we address the fire in the streets and the fire in the mind in the pages ahead, we need to do far more than extinguish a malevolent and destructive blaze. We need to ignite a better fire—one that burns away the dross and gives us the warmth and energy we need to walk wisely, both with the living God and with our neighbor.

SECTION I

HOW THE BLAZE
GOT STARTED

CHAPTER ONE

FIRE IN THE MIND OF KARL MARX AND HIS FOLLOWERS

From Marxism to Critical Race Theory

I t is not name-calling to say that the roots of CRT are found in Marxism. But the issue goes deeper. To some, the label "Marxism" or "Marxist" means little or nothing, since they are ignorant of the philosophy's origins, teachings, and outcomes. This is true for many who did not live as adults through any part of the Cold War between the US and the USSR (1947–1991).[1] This is the generation that knew not Joseph (Stalin).[2] It is largely ignorant about Communism, the ideology that has controlled China and North Korea since 1949, Cuba since 1961, Laos since 1975, and Vietnam since 1976.[3] This means 1.5 billion people are currently enslaved by Marxism.[4]

To some, "Marxism" is a term of appreciation, even a compliment. Black Lives Matter cofounder Patrisse Cullors said that she and fellow founder Alicia Garza were "trained Marxists."[5] By "*trained Marxist,*" she meant that they are activists and organizers, not just thinkers or academics. In fact, the leaders of BLM are the disciples of violent Marxist revolutionaries of the New Left from the 1960s and the violent Black Power movement of the 1970s.[6] In 2015, Garza told *SF Weekly* that "social movements all over the world have used Marx and Lenin as a foundation to interrupt these systems that are really negatively impacting the majority of people."[7] She is continuing that mission; thus, we must critique it.

Marxism 101

Socialism did not originate with the German philosopher Karl Marx (1818–1883), but he gave it a revolutionary and apocalyptic shape that set the world on fire. In his 1872 novel *Demons*, Fyodor Dostoevsky anticipated a kind of revolutionary, even before Marx, who "rejects morality outright, and holds to the newest principle of universal destruction for the sake of good final goals. He's already demanding more than a hundred million heads in order to establish common sense in Europe."[8] Remarkably, the total death toll that Marxist regimes in the twentieth century inflicted on their own people (in Russia, China, Cambodia, North Korea, Cuba, etc.) was more than one hundred million.[9]

Marx was a study in debauchery. Without gainful employment, dependent on his parents until they cut him off (after which he denounced them), a terrible father and husband, and an adulterer, Marx was no epitome of virtue. Added to that, he was a racist (using the N-bomb often)[10] and an antisemite (although he was ethnically Jewish). Marx fashioned himself a demonic figure, a Mephistopheles who cursed Heaven in the name of autonomous and rebellious man.[11] Paul Kengor notes in a piece for the *Epoch Times* that "Marx was particularly fond of a line from Mephistopheles in Goethe's 'Faust': 'Everything that exists deserves to perish.'"[12]

Marx's ruling passion was political revolution. He and his collaborator and patron Frederick Engels (1820–1895) (who, ironically or hypocritically, was a capitalist), let forth onto the world an ideology that stoked the flames of class resentment, fomented a hope for earthly redemption through revolution, and offered a crude account of history, struggle, and destiny summed up in the fiery 1844 pamphlet, *The Communist Manifesto*. As Marx wrote, "Philosophers have hitherto only *interpreted* the world in various ways; the point is to *change* it."[13] His philosophy did change the world, but for the worse—far worse than any other philosophy in history.

We now consider Marxist fundamentals and how Marxism has poisoned history. It holds no promise as a logical worldview, a system of analysis, or as a social program, CRT to the contrary.

First, Marx made atheism central and ineradicable. For him, "the criticism of religion is the prerequisite of all criticism."[14] By "criticism," he means refutation and dismissal. He took religion (primarily Judaism and Christianity) to be a false and disempowering compensation for the political sufferings of this world.[15]

> Religion is the sigh of the oppressed creature, the heart of a heartless world, and the soul of soulless conditions. It is the opium of the people. The abolition of religion as the illusory happiness of the people is the demand for their real happiness.[16]

Religion is nothing but "the flowers on the chains of oppression."[17] It anesthetizes the oppressed, thus rendering them unable to revolt. *The Communist Manifesto* proclaims that:

> Communism abolishes eternal truths, it abolishes all religion, and all morality, instead of constituting them on a new basis; it therefore acts in contradiction to all past historical experience.[18]

Marxism abolishes the fear of God and makes humans their own masters, who can throw off the fetters of oppression and bring about a heaven on Earth.

Ironically, if atheism is true, then Marxism falls flat and hard on its godless face, since all objective value, historical purpose, and social progress is siphoned out of a godless cosmos.[19] Marxism dissolves without its labor theory of *value*. But if the universe is exhausted by matter in motion, then humans are no more *valuable* than anything else, and it all boils down to a pointless quest to survive until death undoes everything. For atheists, everything is devalued or valueless. Moreover, Marx to the contrary, much more goes into economic value than labor, such as relative demand, the costs incurred by manufacturing and development, and other elements.[20]

Second, Marxists believe that history is defined by the relentless struggle between two economic classes: the owners of the means of production (bourgeoisie) and the workers (the proletariat). Marx and Engels offer the master key, writing: "The history of all hitherto existing society is the history of class struggles."[21] This struggle is over economic power and property—that is, over *capital*. Throughout the various economic systems in history, the fundamental antagonism has been between those who own property and the means of production (such as factories) and those who own little or no property and do not own or control the means of production. The owners employ workers, through whom they make a profit (or return on investment). This profit necessarily comes at the expense of the workers, who are thus alienated from the fruits of their labors. This alienation is the central human problem and is socially generated.

This analysis gives Marxism a dramatic narrative of the ongoing life-and-death struggle between the oppressors and the oppressed. Marx and Engels were experts at describing the misery of the poor in the aftermath of the Industrial Revolution and at whipping up outrage over the fate of the impoverished and against the oppressing capitalists. They turned some good phrases in justifying their bad philosophy.

While they were not experts in alleviating any of these problems, Marx and Engels—along with their totalitarian followers, such as Vladimir Lenin (Russia), Joseph Stalin (Russia), Mao Zedong (China), Pol Pot (Cambodia), and Fidel Castro (Cuba)—were experts on fomenting violent revolution, destabilizing society, impoverishing the masses (often through famine), oppressing citizens, disallowing elections, and killing millions upon millions of their own people during "peacetime." But private property was the real culprit in human misery. Marx wrote:

> Under private property... [e]ach tries to establish over the other an alien power, so as thereby to find satisfaction of his own selfish need. The increase in the quantity of objects is therefore accompanied by an extension of the realm of the alien powers to which man is subjected, and every new product represents a new potentiality of mutual swindling and mutual plundering.[22]

Notice that phrase "alien powers," which is crucial and central for Marxism. All profit alienates the workers who contributed to the profit enjoyed by the owners. But while profits in some cases may be exorbitant, they are not intrinsically alienating, since profits allow owners to further develop their business, hire more workers, and provide more services. None of Marx's key ideas were testable. As economist (and ex-Marxist) Thomas Sowell observes in his analysis of Marx's three-volume tome, *Kapital*:

> "[E]xploitation" was at no point in its 2,500 pages treated as a testable hypothesis. Exploitation was instead the

foundation assumption on which an elaborate intellectual superstructure was built—and that proved to be a foundation of quicksand. Getting rid of capitalist "exploiters" in Communist countries did not raise the living standards of workers even to levels common in many capitalist countries, where workers were presumably still being exploited, as Marxists conceived the term.[23]

Marx's idea of "exploitation" could not be confirmed. However, the egregious effects of his system have *falsified* his claims that Marxism betters a society.

Third, the Marxist vision is that of *revolting against*, not of reforming, existing society. A revolution means the total overthrow and replacement of social, political, and economic structures. The capitalist order is intrinsically oppressive to the workers and must be abolished along with all that flows from that capitalist order, such as the traditional family. Marxists hold that the most taken-for-granted institutions were based on exploitation. Of course, private property had to be abolished and expropriated by the communist state, and along with it, the traditional family had to be abolished as well.

On what foundation is the present family, the bourgeois family, based? On capital, on private gain. In its completely developed form this family exists only among the bourgeoisie. But this state of things finds its complement in the practical absence of the family among the proletarians, and in public prostitution. The bourgeois family will vanish as a matter of course when its complement vanishes, and both will vanish with the vanishing of capital.[24]

The family, wherein heterosexual parents raise their children, is known in every society and under every economic condition. This is because it is ordained as such by God (Genesis 1–2; Matthew 19:1–6). But the family poses a threat to the Marxists and to neo-Marxists (such as CRT advocates), since it is a unit of power, fidelity, and tradition that resists the overthrow of society through revolution.

Fourth, Marxism is fueled by a futuristic vision of victory for the oppressed masses. After the capitalist order is overthrown, the "dictatorship of the proletariat" will result, in which all bourgeoise values will be swept away through the coercive power of the newly liberated proletariat. In one of the most egregiously false and ironic statements ever made in philosophy, Marxism claims that after this dictatorship, the state would "wither away," leading to the communist society.[25] Nothing of the sort has ever happened under any Marxist government. It can never happen under any form of civil government because Marxism is impotent to change our fallen human nature and its effects, as is any merely human philosophy (Colossians 2:8).

No dictatorship will usher in its own demise and give birth to a society so perfect that it needs no civil government. Civil government is required to keep a measure of order in a fallen world, as the Bible affirms (Romans 13:1–7; 1 Peter 2:13–17), even though it easily and often goes astray in its quest for unaccountable power, as the Bible warns (1 Samuel 8; Acts 12:19–23; Revelation 13).

According to Marxism, through the necessary conflicts between classes over ages, the economic forces of history will culminate in a classless and stateless society in which the division of labor no longer obtains. Marx waxed rhapsodic about this future communist state.

> Nobody has one exclusive sphere of activity but each can become accomplished in any branch he wishes, society

regulates the general production and thus makes it possible for me to do one thing today and another tomorrow, to hunt in the morning, fish in the afternoon, rear cattle in the evening, criticise after dinner, just as I have a mind, without ever becoming hunter, fisherman, herdsman or critic.[26]

This is undiluted and rhapsodic utopianism. There is literally "no place" like it in a world still groaning for its final redemption (Romans 8:18–26). Rather than chronicling the horrific effects of Marxism in nation after nation, I will simply refer to the earlier statement that Marxist regimes are credited with the killing of more than one hundred million (100,000,000) of their own citizens—a practice that the late political scientist R. J. Rummel called *democide*, which "means for governments what murder means for an individual under municipal law. It is the premeditated killing of a person in cold blood or causing the death of a person through reckless and wanton disregard for their life."[27] No one has exceeded the Marxists in this deadly skill.

Enter Critical Theory

Marxism became mainstream in America through a long, slow process. Antonio Gramsci (1891–1937), an Italian Communist, wrote of the need for Marxism to infiltrate institutions gradually and over time, instead of waging a cataclysmic revolution.[28] Marxism has indeed marched through our institutions; the academic world has been particularly affected. In 1989, the *New York Times* reported: "As Karl Marx's ideological heirs in Communist nations struggle to transform his political legacy, his intellectual heirs on American campuses have virtually completed their own transformation from brash, beleaguered outsiders to assimilated academic insiders."[29] I have witnessed this throughout my secular education.

In 1923, the Institute for Social Research was founded in Frankfurt, Germany. According to philosopher Stephen Bronner, it was a "Marxist study group" which "sought to deal with the practical problems facing the labor movement in the aftermath of the Russian Revolution."[30] This came to be known as the Frankfurt School. Its "inner circle" included Max Horkheimer (a philosopher and the group's principal organizer and leader), psychologist Erich Fromm, social critic Walter Benjamin, philosopher Theodor Adorno, and, most significantly because of his influence, philosopher Herbert Marcuse, who would help shape Critical Theory into Critical *Race* Theory.[31]

The term "Critical Theory" was coined in 1937 when the Frankfurters found sanctuary in America after their Marxism put them in danger in Germany.[32] The name "Critical Theory" covered for Marxism; but they offered a Marxism willing to adapt to current circumstances in the West and especially in America.

> Critical theory was intended as a general theory of society fueled by the desire for liberation. Its practitioners understood that new social conditions would give rise to new ideas and new problems for radical practice—and that the character of the critical method would change along with the substance of emancipation.[33]

Those in the Frankfurt School, atheists to a man, extended their critique of oppression beyond economic categories (the workers against the owners) to include cultural factors related to race, gender, and sexuality. In classical Marxism, the economic base determined the cultural superstructure. Hence, economics explains nearly everything.

But for the members of the Frankfurt School, the superstructure of culture had to be addressed in its own right, since bourgeoise culture is deceptive and must be unmasked and debunked in order for revolution to result.

The Frankfurters realized that Marx's predictions that the workers would overthrow the owners had not occurred anywhere. The Russian Revolution was not a peasant revolt, but led by elitists such as Lenin. Stalin, no peasant himself, would later starve about four million Ukrainian peasants when these farmers refused to give up their small parcels of land to the collective. This called forth Stalin's "planned famine" from 1932–33.[34]

One Frankfurter will detain us: Herbert Marcuse (1898–1979), the leading philosopher of the New Left and formidable influence on CRT. Among other things, he mentored Angela Davis,[35] who is herself a mentor to Black Lives Matter leaders.[36]

Marcuse was born in Germany but established a successful academic career in the United States after fleeing Nazism.[37] He was a prolific author who gained fame with *One Dimensional Man* (1964).[38] Marcuse was an inspiration for the campus protests of the 1960s in America and especially in France in 1968, when college students painted statements from his books on walls as intellectual graffiti.

Marcuse's key contribution to Marxism was his incorporation of Freudian psychoanalytical themes into a revolutionary program. He expanded the base for social revolution to include not only oppressed workers (an economic factor), but also those considered to be sexual or social deviants no matter what their economic class (a cultural factor), and those in minority groups (a racial factor). Thus, he called for homosexuals, lesbians, bisexuals, and those in other nontraditional sexual categories to join the revolution against the capitalist-traditional-family status quo. In *Eros and Civilization: A Philosophical Inquiry into Freud*, a 1959 bestseller, he writes that the body can be freed from monogamous constraints to find full erotic experience.[39] Marcuse called for a "polymorphous" sexuality— one not limited by bourgeoise traditions of repression.

The hedonistic counterculture of the 1960s was happy to oblige Marcuse with its motto of "sex, drugs, and rock and roll." The slogan, "Make love, not war," probably traces to Marcuse as well, who opposed the United States' war in Vietnam as the result of capitalism's inevitable imperialism. However ill-conceived or ill-executed, it was a war prosecuted to counter Communist aggression. But Marxist ideology blames capitalism for nearly all ills, domestic and international.[40]

For Marcuse, "a one-dimensional man" is anesthetized by material comforts and the blandishments of technological society. He must be roused from his capitalist torpor in order to discern his underlying discontent. Marcuse strained to explain Marx's failed prophecy that the struggle between the bourgeois and proletariat would lead to revolution by claiming that "technological rationality" had somehow tamed the workers to make an unacknowledged pact with the owners. Now Marcuse would rip open the wound and reveal the disease.[41]

Such is the central and vexing problem for critical theorists.[42] Accordingly, Marcuse and his ilk had to dig deeper to find alienation-subjugation and to sell the stimulant for liberation—even after the economic boom of post-war America, even after the civil rights advances of the 1950s and 1960s. For Marcuse, the freedoms of "pluralist democracy"—consider the five freedoms of the First Amendment—and the material benefits of "extravagant productivity" are merely veils that cover an "expansive apparatus of exploitation."[43] This works itself out in imperialistic wars (Vietnam) and in sexual inhibition.

Like all Marxists, Marcuse viewed the traditional family as an engine of oppression and as an impediment to revolution. While Marx and Engels called for the abolition of the bourgeois family in *The*

Communist Manifesto, they did not advocate homosexuality, lesbianism, or bisexuality—let alone same-sex marriage. That was left to Marcuse, the New Left, the counterculture, and subsequent CRT advocates.

Besides appealing to sexual minorities, Marcuse appeals to POC to join the revolution against capitalism, since he, like today's CRT proponents, deemed capitalism to be supporting racism. He writes, "Underneath the conservative popular base is the substratum of the outcasts and outsiders, the exploited and persecuted of other races and other colors."[44] The USSR worked hard in the United States to recruit African Americans and other minorities to their cause, claiming that their plight was rooted in the exploitation of the capitalists. They had only mixed success up until the 1960s.[45] But that would change.

Derrick Bell and Critical Race Theory

Derrick Bell (1930–2011) considered racial bias in our legal system—a worthy goal, if done well. He was a prominent civil rights attorney for the NAACP Legal Defense Fund and the first black person to become a tenured law professor at Harvard in 1971. His ideas have shaped CRT significantly, as well as influencing a young Barack Obama, who was one of his students at Harvard Law School and who assigned some of Bell's writings while he was a professor at the University of Chicago Law School.[46]

I will further critique Bell's claims about systemic racism later in this book, but I will briefly mention his significance for CRT. He claimed that American law remained racist even after the Civil Rights gains of the 1950s and 1960s. This racism is "permanent" and systemic in the United States, and white people only agree to help black people when it helps them. The assessment of law and politics must shift away from objective concerns based on empirical evidence to black people's "lived experience." This quote explains the approach of CRT thinkers and advocates today.

> We believe that standards and institutions created by and fortifying white power ought to be resisted.... We insist, for example, that abstraction, put forth as "rational" or "objective" truth, smuggles the privileged choice of the privileged to depersonify their claims and then pass them off as the universal authority and the universal good. To counter such assumptions, we try to bring to legal scholarship an experientially grounded, oppositionally expressed, and transformatively aspirational concern with race and other socially constructed hierarchies.[47]

The Marxist themes are transparent. Here is my translation of the turgid prose: "We do not play by rules set down by the oppressors, but forge our own critique, which is shielded from criticism because we must struggle against these oppressors. We do not win arguments, but discredit our opponents, who are nothing but power-mongering and privileged oppressors." Bell commonly committed the fallacy of poisoning the well when criticized by white writers who, he claimed, simply wanted to maintain their dominance.[48]

Marxism and Cultural Marxism

This chapter attempts to show that CRT is not only rooted in Marxism, but is a racially charged development of Marxist themes. That Marxist root is rotten, considering the Marxist history of oppression, expropriation, and political murder on an unthinkable scale. Marx's fundamental assumptions about God, humanity, and value were false. The central error consists in deeming human society in strictly binary terms—oppressors and oppressed—and with no possibility of reform according to classically liberal principles, such as free speech, individual rights, and limited government. Both original Marxism and cultural Marxism (CRT) are revolutionary at their core and seek nothing less than the total transformation of society in their socialist-statist image.

Summarizing the relationship between Marxism and CRT is a fitting way to end this chapter.

Orthodox Marxists look to Marx, Engels, and Lenin as their philosophical and political inspiration, as do CRT advocates; but the latter add the ideas of Critical Theory and Critical Legal Studies as well. Nevertheless, the roots are identical.

They both divide the world into oppressors and oppressed, a radical dichotomy from which their entire worldview springs.

They both claim they alone possess the vantage point from which society can be understood.

They both claim that the oppressors—defined as the bourgeoise (for Marxists) or as those in league with white supremacy (for CRT)—are hopelessly hoodwinked by their biases, prejudices, and privileges from seeing reality as it is. They must be reeducated or silenced, or worse. (See my discussion of ideology in Chapter Five.)

They both view themselves as the only vanguard from which meaningful change (revolution) will come.

They both employ an "ends justify the means" or "by any means necessary" mentality to achieve their goals. Abiding moral principles such as nonviolence, truth-telling, or free speech may be sacrificed for the sake of the Cause.

Today, it is CRT, and not so much classical Marxism, that is in the headlines and which is taken to the streets to shout, loot, and burn. But from Marxist roots, no good fruit may come. So, we move on to challenge CRT through fact, logic, and evidence.

Much is at stake, even America herself.

CHAPTER TWO

FIRE IN OUR OWN HOUSE

The fires of extremism need to be extinguished, and the fires of a
better vision need to warm and light up our cultural landscape.
To do so, we may need to overcome obstacles that keep us from wisely
engaging the pressing moral issues of the day, especially related to
CRT. However, we may be caught flatfooted and with our heads in
the clouds. When asked to speak, we may put our foot in our mouth.
While the following chapters will consider specific issues in depth,
this one addresses preliminary matters of orientation to our present
crisis. To counter the fire in the streets, we need the right kind of fire
in our own hearts and minds. Thus, we will address the problems of
apathy, media awareness, and collective white guilt.

An Apathy Epidemic

While tens of thousands protested and rioted in the summer of
2020, many were stunned and caught off guard. No one could have

predicted the apocalyptic aftermath of George Floyd's death; nonetheless, the fires of revolution had been burning for years in the minds of academics and activists. CRT did not pop up out of nothing, but rather found a conduit for its ideas by giving rage a militant mindset that had been present for decades. (I touched on this in the last chapter, and it will be further explained in the following chapters.) Too many Americans were intellectually apathetic about the plate tectonic shifts that had taken place in the philosophy of race and politics.

A turning point was the presidency of Barack Obama who, while he presented himself as a moderate, was in reality an advocate of CRT and black liberation theology as taught in his church by his pastor, Jeremiah Wright. Dr. Wright officiated the Obamas' wedding ceremony, baptized their two daughters, often denounced America, and shouted in a 2003 sermon, "Not God bless America, but God damn America."[1] Obama began his political career with the support of William Ayers and Bernardine Dohrn, who were violent activists of the New Left in the 1970s and responsible for many bombings across the country. They were part of a band of "bomb-throwing Marxists" called the Weather Underground that terrorized America.[2] They later became "tenured radicals" who have never renounced their revolutionary violence.[3]

Obama's subsequent policies bore out his influences, although he moderated them. Gifted with charisma and challenged by two weak and white establishment candidates for the presidency, Obama easily swept into office and stayed there for two terms. Many who were delighted to see the first black man in the White House neglected to look beneath his skin to find his ruling passions and past alliances.[4]

Two presidents after Obama, apathy is no longer an option. As I write this book in late 2021, contentment is ebbing, given the ongoing global pandemic, runaway inflation, shortages of goods, employment shortfalls, an illegal immigration crisis, a drug crisis, and more. But too many Americans think that America has eternal security, that its laurels are sufficient for its future. Francis Schaeffer warned of this in 1976, and his warning is worth hearing again.

> As the more Christian-dominated consensus weakened, the majority of people adopted two impoverished values: personal peace and affluence. Personal peace means just to be let alone, not to be troubled by the troubles of other people, whether across the world or across the city—to live one's life with minimal possibilities of being personally disturbed. Personal peace means wanting to have my personal life pattern undisturbed in my lifetime, regardless of what the result will be in the lifetimes of my children and grandchildren. Affluence means an overwhelming and ever-increasing prosperity—a life made up of things, things, and more things—a success judged by an ever-higher level of material abundance.[5]

The foundations of American greatness are shaking, but no matter how grim the situation or how dire the prospects for a nation, a holy God sits above it all, examining both good and evil; and He will act in His good time to judge the wicked and reward the righteous (Psalm 11). All of our thinking and acting should be predicated on these living truths. Otherwise, we will fall into panic, desperation, and ill-advised actions.

A Primer on Media Awareness

It is impossible to form reasonable beliefs and coherent action plans about our social upheaval without being media savvy. We must weigh ideas for truth: "In a lawsuit the first to speak seems right, until someone comes forward and cross-examines" (Proverbs 18:17). It was said of "the tribe of Issachar" that "understood the times and knew what Israel should do" (1 Chronicles 12:32). The Apostle Peter said of King David that he "served God's purpose in his own generation" (Acts 13:36). He discerned God's purpose and acted accordingly. Anyone who wants to gain knowledge about CRT and a better alternative to the issues that it raises needs to ardently pursue truth, especially if one is a teacher or writer (Malachi 2:7–8; James 3:1–3; Titus 2:7–8). So here is a crash course on media discernment.

First, we require self-discipline in seeking truth. It is too easy to be blown about by every wind of opinion (Ephesians 4:4). Discerning truth from falsity demands wisdom, patience, and prayer. The Book of Hebrews scolds and chastens its readers for their immaturity when they should know more and know better. They were at a cognitive standstill and were intellectually infantile—needing milk, not meat. "But solid food is for the mature, who by constant use have trained themselves to distinguish good from evil" (Hebrews 5:14).

To gain wisdom, we must not waste time. In 1985, Neil Postman warned that we were "amusing ourselves to death" and thus losing the moral seriousness needed for a conscientious life.[6] How much more now. Any serious student of culture and politics must refuse to gorge on entertainment (particularly video games, fantasy sports, binge-watching TV shows) since time need be spent in research and analysis. As Moses wrote, "Teach us to number our days, that we may gain a heart of wisdom" (Psalm 90:12; see also Ephesians 5:16).

Second, every medium, by its very nature, shapes its message and should be judged accordingly.[7] Electronic media trade on images more than words. A picture may be worth a thousand words, but pictures lack the specificity of words. Even a nonabstract painting of a specific thing, such as mountain, does not affirm anything, although much may be said about it. But the statement, "A riot occurred in Kenosha, Wisconsin today," has a specified verbal meaning, which is either true or false. Many different images could be used to cover the riot, and all of them are edited. Seeing may be believing, but vision has its limits as well, since what you see may not accurately reflect reality. Which part of the riot was filmed? Why did the people riot? These questions cannot be captured by images accompanied by minimal comment.[8]

Third, media affect not only the information we receive, but how we relate to reality. As Marshall McLuhan said, "We become what we behold. We shape our tools and our tools shape us." This comment was inspired by the Psalmist, who wrote: "But their idols are silver and gold, made by human hands.... Those who make them will be like them, and so will all who trust in them" (Psalm 115:4, 8).

If we become accustomed to understanding the world through a half-hour national news report, then we may uncritically believe that two- or three-minute stories on television give an accurate depiction of reality.[9] If the news anchor looks convincing and has a pleasant voice, we trust him or her, even though this has nothing to do with his or her veracity.[10] But a half-hour program is an eon for many because their attention spans are defined by even shorter bursts from Twitter, Facebook, Instagram, and YouTube. In *The Shallows*, author Nicholas Carr confesses that after several years of spending more time online than reading books, his attention span shortened. Protracted exposure to screens literally changes the shape of our brains, and our cognitive and perceptual sensitivities with it.[11]

Fourth, beware of advocacy journalism. No journalist is perfectly fair in all things, but many have given up trying. Some media are dominated by an ideology that ruins objectivity.[12] Their news stories are editorials, and their editorials represent only one viewpoint.[13] Indeed, journalism is currently rife with discussions about whether seeking to present "objective truth" should even still be a goal, given that everyone now has their "lived experience" by which to judge reality; rather, these advocates say, facts should only be presented that support the goal of reforming culture. This is not very surprising, considering that the legacy news media in the United States are dominated by a left-leaning, pro-CRT perspective.[14] That does not make them entirely unreliable, however. Conservative media, such as Fox News or Newsmax, may not give all pertinent sides to their reporting and editorializing either, and they often hurl unneeded invectives just as the hosts on CNN and MSNBC do.

Fifth, choosing sources for knowledge is an art acquired over time more than a science, but general principles emerge.[15] Books published by established public companies are to be trusted more than self-published books, since the former are vetted by outside sources and the latter are not. Of course, well-established publishers are responsible for many of the CRT ideas I reject, so other judgments are needed. When considering a book, evaluate the author's credentials. Also check to see who has endorsed the book and what their credentials are.

Magazines and journals may give in-depth perspective on matters of race, gender, politics, and related topics, but need to be judged by their longevity, reputation, and authors. Some periodicals are specific in their viewpoints. You will never find a pro-free market article in *The Nation*, nor a defense of socialism at *National Review*. You won't find an article or editorial critical of CRT or BLM in the *New York Times*. Reading essays and reviews on different sides of issues helps develop your critical faculties.

The internet makes the Wild West look tame in comparison, given its profligate information, its lack of filters, its ability to generate or revive absurd ideas (such as the flat earth and QAnon nonsense, and more), its endless debates, its tidal wave of trivia, and its overt propaganda. However, it also hosts reliable sources and is a treasure trove of useful facts when used well. A blog is not generally as reliable as a published article, but a blog by a credentialed expert may be worthwhile. Wikipedia is a place to start serious research, but not a place to stop. Most Wikipedia entries have links to more reliable sources, such as books, journals, and magazines. Those should be consulted as more authoritative, but not Wikipedia itself, since it is anonymous, crowd-sourced, and ever-changeable. Editing is minimal and sporadic, and often done by those with overt agendas. YouTube videos are a mixed bag, depending on the credibility of the speaker. Some people are good at making YouTube videos and getting huge followings, but have inadequate credentials. (This is akin to Daniel Boorstin's observations in *The Image* that celebrities are people "well known for their well-knownness."[16])

To train our skills, we will consider the epicenter of unrest: George Floyd.

The George Floyd Video

The video of George Floyd went viral on March 20, 2020. A few minutes of dramatic images were taken largely out of context and used as the interpretive grid according to a preset narrative. Until more facts were revealed later, I too was caught up in the image of police brutality due to racism against a black man. But that was not entirely true, despite the thousands of protests and the widespread rioting that resulted in mass carnage and terror in the United States.

The story was predetermined: a poor and troubled black man is harshly treated by a white police officer, who literally has his knee on his neck while the black man cries out, "I can't breathe!" Floyd dies under that knee. To many, it all was deeply symbolic of white supremacy over black people through force of law and hate. However, if "seeing is believing," we need to ask, "Seeing what and in what context in order to believe what?"

As we later learned, George Floyd was not an innocent man, however wrongly he may have been treated. He had a long history of crime, including felonies and long jail time.[17] His encounter with the police came after a cashier reported that he tried to pass a phony twenty-dollar bill at a grocery store. During the tussle with police, Floyd was dazed and acting erratically due to a potentially lethal dose of fentanyl in his body. He could not, or did not, follow police instructions, and he resisted arrest. The officers tried to contain him in a police car, but since he claimed he was claustrophobic (despite having arrived at the store in a car), they let him out. *Before* he was put into the compliance hold by Officer Derek Chauvin, he had been exclaiming, "I can't breathe!" repeatedly and calling for his mother. The compliance hold was not *meant* to choke him—let alone kill him. A prosecutor specializing in police brutality cases reported in the *American Spectator*, "Minnesota police are trained to use a 'neck restraint' technique, which is defined in the official training literature as 'compressing one or both sides of a person's neck with an arm or leg, without applying direct pressure to the trachea or airway (front of the neck).' The video of Chauvin kneeling on the side of Floyd's neck appears to be a textbook application of this officially approved technique."[18] While it looked like Floyd was intentionally suffocated, that is questionable. The police had called an ambulance before Floyd was put into the compliance hold, but he was dead when it arrived.

Given the mass outrage at the event, it is unlikely that Chauvin got a fair trial. The whole world had already convicted him of murder before the full evidence was available. A change of venue was needed for the trial, given the local outrage, but was not granted. The jury was not adequately sequestered, and the jurors knew they would have been harmed or killed had they not rendered a murder verdict.[19] Thus, the jury was unlikely to be objective or fair. I am not saying Chauvin was innocent, but I am highlighting pertinent facts that are often overlooked given the power of the CRT ideology and people's inability to weigh media sources carefully.

What many people missed was this: That a black man dying while under police custody while a white man restrained him does not *automatically imply racism* as a motive in George Floyd's death. However guilty Chauvin may have been—and he was sentenced severely—racism was never established. Minnesota Attorney General Keith Ellison, who is black and on the far left, was in charge of Chauvin's prosecution and responsible for criminal charges. When interviewed on CBS's *60 Minutes*, Ellison denied that George Floyd was a victim of a "hate crime" or racial bias. "I wouldn't call it that because hate crimes are crimes where there's an explicit motive and bias," Ellison said. "We don't have any evidence that Derek Chauvin factored in George Floyd's race as he did what he did." He also said that Minnesota decided to not convict for a hate crime because "we only charge those crimes that we had evidence that we could put in front of a jury to prove."[20]

Essential principles and precedents of our legal system were swept aside in this case—that the defendant is innocent until proven guilty beyond a reasonable doubt, and that the defendant receive a fair trial through due process. The mob had spoken, and the case was closed before it opened. This is not good for America.

Knowing the Larger Context

The emotional and literal explosions that followed the release of the George Floyd video did not occur in a vacuum, but rather in the already-lit fire of a narrative that America is systemically racist and America's police are often antiblack and unfairly target black people for arrest, harassment, and death.

There is no question that African Americans have been mistreated by police because of racism over the years. Consider the fire hoses and dogs used against Martin Luther King and his followers and the routine police beatings of black people in the South before the Civil Rights Movement, or the lack of proper legal representation given to some black people today.[21] However, today, each case must be judged individually. Fixed narratives should not overwhelm the facts on the ground.

The fury over police treatment of black people began to build with the death of Michael Brown in Ferguson, Missouri, in 2014. A young black man was "caught by security cameras at a local store overpowering an Asian shopkeeper who was half his size, shoving him with great force, and stealing Swisher Sweets cigars off his counter."[22] The police were called, and Brown was confronted by an officer. He then resisted arrest to the point of trying to grab the officer's gun. After he fled, he turned back and charged the officer, who fatally shot him, since he feared for his life. Brown was 6'4" and 294 pounds, an imposing physical presence.

While the officer was not convicted of wrongdoing, a narrative emerged on the street that Brown had been "executed" by the officer while holding his hands up and saying, "Hands up. Don't shoot." Protests sometimes turned violent and the city was in an uproar. After the local courts cleared the officer, President Obama sent in his Attorney General, Eric Holder (a black man), to investigate. That federal investigation agreed with the state judgment: not guilty. Nevertheless, the Ferguson event was used to galvanize a narrative of systemic police violence against black people. This in turn produced "the Ferguson effect." As author Heather Mac Donald notes:

> Officers backed off proactive policing in minority neighborhoods, having been told that such discretionary enforcement was racially oppressive. By early 2015, the resulting spike in shootings and homicides had become patent and

would lead to an additional 2,000 black homicide victims in 2015 and 2016, compared with 2014 numbers.[23]

This worsened considerably after Floyd's death, with frequent calls to "defund the police"—just when policing was so necessary to quell violence and protect people and property.[24] Police reforms are one thing; defunding an institution necessary because of the Fall of humanity is something else—a dangerous proposal. After the hysteria, some who clambered for defunding realized, in light of soaring crime rates, that the police needed to be refunded. For example, "In New York City, Mayor Bill de Blasio said he would reinstate $92 million for a new precinct after scrapping the project last summer."[25] Common sense strikes back.

John McWhorter, a Columbia University linguistic professor who is black, speaks a simple truth: "I heartily espouse police reform but consider it unlikely that anything can be done to stop cops from firing their weapons lethally in tight or even risky situations."[26] He emphasizes black responsibility when he says that "changing the cops will take eons; changing black lives should take less time than that."[27]

I could go on about police killings of black people, and again, each case must be assessed individually; but I will refer the reader to in-depth sources.[28] In the meantime, consider this comment from Wilfred Reilly, a political scientist who is black:

There is no violent genocide against African Americans currently going on: both FBI and Bureau of Justice Statistics data indicate that interracial violent crime is fairly rare—and roughly 80 percent Black on white. The total number of people shot by police officers, a particular focus of Black Lives Matter, was under 1,200 in the

representative year of 2015, and 76 percent of the individuals shot were not black.[29]

The upshot is that we should not be quick to jump on any band-
wagon, no matter how many others do. Sowell is right to say that
there "is something obscene about judges and journalists nit-picking
at leisure, and in safety and comfort, a life-and-death decision that
some policeman had a split second to make."[30] Megaphones and
marching—let alone torching—do not create facts or give reliable
interpretations. We need cool heads in this hot furnace.

Racism and White Guilt

Racism is morally wrong. Unjust prejudice against groups and
bias toward one's race is immoral. There is but one human race, created by God (Genesis 1:26). We all bear the image of God as our
essential and ineradicable identity, whatever differences there are
among us. How do we assess and address moral guilt?

As philosopher R. J. Rushdoony notes, "The roots of guilt are
personal and racial; the consequences are social as well. The human
race, in apostasy from God, is deeply involved in a rebellious claim
to autonomy and in the guilt which follows that claim."[31] Ever since,
conscience has been troubled or cleared; moral accusations have been
made (rightly or wrongly); excuses (good and bad) have been offered;
laws (just and unjust) have been framed (which have either been
enforced or unenforced); moral philosophers have debated innocence
and guilt; and mortals East of Eden have staggered along—sometimes
spotting the moral lodestar, sometimes missing it.

With matters of guilt come questions of atonement and punishment. Humans are guilty of many misdeeds and many vices. We

experience what the late theologian Francis Schaeffer called "true moral guilt."

> All men are separated from God because of their true moral guilt. God exists, God has a character, God is a holy God; and when men sin (and we all must acknowledge we have sinned not only by mistake but by intention), they have true moral guilt before the God who exists. That guilt is not just the modern concept of guilt-feelings, a psychological guilty feeling in man. It is a true moral guilt before the infinite-personal, holy God.[32]

We sin and incur true moral guilt before God, and no one (spare Christ) is excepted, since "all have sinned and fall short of the glory of God" (Romans 3:23). Our primary guilt is before God and against God (Matthew 22:37). Added to that is guilt for not loving our neighbors as we ought (Matthew 22:38).

The first issue concerning guilt and innocence is moral evaluation, starting with oneself. Accusations of guilt fly around the world wildly at the speed of the internet, and reckless shaming is common. But what matters is objective reality based on facts and principles.

Jesus realized that we habitually find fault in others without applying that fault-finding standard to ourselves. If so, we are hypocrites who should repent. If we repent, then our moral vision becomes less clouded, and we may discern reality aright. This is true of moral matters pertaining to race and to everything else (Matthew 7:3–5). Our moral judgments—about race or anything else—should be carefully considered and start with self. As Jesus commanded the Pharisees after a discussion about the morality of the Sabbath, "Stop judging by mere appearances, but instead judge correctly" (John 7:24).

In politics, it is tempting to divide the world into an "us and them" dichotomy with "us" on the right side and "them" on the wrong side. To some degree, this is unavoidable if we are convinced our views on important matters are correct. Nevertheless, we do well to remember the words of Aleksandr Solzhenitsyn (1918–2008), the courageous Russian dissident and author, against the egregious and systemic evils of the communist Soviet Union. After soul-searching in a camp of political prisoners, he wrote:

> Gradually it was disclosed to me that the line separating good and evil passes not through states, nor between classes, nor between political parties either—but right through every human heart—and through all human hearts. This line shifts. Inside us, it oscillates with the years. And even within hearts overwhelmed by evil, one small bridgehead of good is retained. And even in the best of all hearts, there remains… an unuprooted small corner of evil.[33]

The final and ultimate division of humanity—into the redeemed and the unredeemed—can be made by the Almighty alone and will only be revealed and rendered infallibly and inexorably at the Final Judgment (Daniel 12:2; Matthew 7:21–23; 25:31–46; Acts 17:31; Revelation 20:11-15). Until then, as Jesus said, the wheat and the weeds grow together: "Let both grow together until the harvest. At that time I will tell the harvesters: 'First collect the weeds and tie them in bundles to be burned; then gather the wheat and bring it into my barn'" (Matthew 13:30).

How might we determine guilt, punishment, and justice on a social level? If you steal a hundred dollars from me, you are guilty and I am robbed. If a boss passes over a black man for a position to which he is entitled because he is black, then that boss is guilty. But how are societies to be judged as guilty? How might a society make amends? Let us turn to atonement, an inescapable element of human life.

The term *atonement* can mean different things, given the context. But the core meaning is that of appeasing punishment and restoring justice though some deliberate action. The quest for atonement comes from a guilty conscience or from a wounded victim; it is a quest for absolution or a demand for punishment. Rushdoony observes:

> Atonement thus is a repair of the breach caused by guilt, and the consequence of atonement is justification. Because the need for this repair is so urgent, the whole personal, social, religious, and political life of guilty man is colored by this demand for atonement and is in fact dominated by it.[34]

Thus, the question of guilt, atonement, and justification is not only of theological concern, but of social welfare as well.

One hopeless means of seeking atonement is through masochism. This is a form of "self-atonement and self-justification."[35] It differs radically from repentance and making amends, whether that be an apology, restitution, or some means of settling the score. The American Psychological Association defines masochism in this way:

> The derivation of pleasure from experiencing pain and humiliation. The term generally denotes sexual masochism but is also applied to experiences not involving sex....In classical psychoanalytic theory, masochism is interpreted as resulting from the death instinct or from aggression turned inward because of excessive guilt feelings.[36]

One need not hold to Freudian psychoanalytical theory to understand that masochism is often tied to guilt feelings, whether or not those feelings are appropriate. Such pathology is not limited to suicide, cutting oneself, eating disorders, or other physical mutilations, but can even be expressed through political theory and political action. For example, one may give lavishly to a cause to try to atone for wrongs he has done related to the purpose of that charity or cause. If a wealthy white male thinks he is part of a systemically racist and white supremacist society and the unworthy recipient of white privilege, he may contribute large sums to BLM or even Antifa, an openly violent group.

Given the millions of dollars given to BLM by corporations mostly controlled by white men, it appears that these are attempts at self-atonement. I advert to Rushdoony again. Self-atonement of any kind

> is an impossibility, metaphysically and morally. Man is God's creature, totally God's creation, and man can exist only in God's world. He is totally morally liable to God, and man's every attempt to assert a claim to autonomy is not only a violation of his moral duty but a metaphysical impossibility and a mental monstrosity. Man cannot make atonement to God for his sin because he is neither capable of truly self-righteous atonement, since he is nothing in and of himself, nor can he add anything to God.[37]

Far better than any impotent attempt to atone for one's sin or justify oneself through masochism is to have one's sins truly atoned for by Jesus Christ. "He is the atoning sacrifice for our sins, and not only for ours but also for the sins of the whole world" (1 John 2:2). If we accept this, we can begin to see the world aright and live rightly.

Black historian and author Shelby Steele has written widely and wisely on what he calls "white guilt" and how it hobbles prudent politics and hinders sound judgments.[38] Those who suffer from this malady think they have lost moral authority in light of the sweeping changes from the Civil Rights Movement. White people were outed and ashamed after Jim Crow had been legally (if not culturally) discredited through the Civil Rights Act (1964) and *Brown v. Board of Education* (1954). How might white people now navigate through racial issues with this load of guilt?

Steele argues that once the civil rights victories were won, white liberals shifted their emphasis from nondiscrimination against, and freedom for, black people (equal opportunity) to a compensatory approach that assuaged their ongoing racial guilt and vaunted themselves as white saviors of the still-oppressed black people. Instead of maintaining equal access and opportunity for them, the liberals switched to what Steele calls "interventionism"—state-mandated programs to address discrepancies between white and black achievement. He believes that intervention reached the point that even after the civil rights advances, "blacks were still seen as determined beings without will or agency, and therefore without full humanity."[39] On this view, "victimization [became] a totalistic explanation of black difficulty" and "it changed the basic terms of American liberalism from freedom, rights, and responsibilities to planning, engineering, and entitlements."[40]

The CRT and BLM vision for America is to radically restructure institutions in order to achieve "equity"—equal outcomes for POC, whether or not it is accompanied by equal effort. That demands even more "planning, engineering, and entitlements," all coming from the top down through civil government. As the late sociologist Nathan Glazer put it, the emphasis shifted from "equal opportunity to statistical parity."[41] Instead of leveling the playing field and removing obstacles to

achievement, the white liberals viewed black people as unable to achieve
their goals without special treatment through extensive governmental
assistance. Steele takes this to be condescending.

> Double standards, preferential treatment, provisions for
> "cultural difference," and various kinds of entitlement all
> constitute a pattern of exceptionalism that keeps blacks
> (and other minorities) down by tolerating weakness at
> every juncture where strength is expected of others.[42]

While not denying the racist guilt of many white people, especially
under slavery and Jim Crow, Steele denies that America is now a
systemically racist nation. As such, white guilt should not be a moti-
vating force in political or cultural life.[43] We have come too far, he
claims, and he has perspective. Steele often accompanied his father,
a truck driver, to civil rights protests in the 1960s, and so experienced
the realities of racism himself as the son of a black father and a white
mother. He was seriously involved in the Black Power movement
before becoming disenchanted with big government programs to help
blacks and changing his mind about leftist views on race. He voted
for black leftist Jesse Jackson in 1984 and 1988.[44]

White Privilege

CRT advocates and those like-minded accuse white people of
benefitting from "white privilege," and thus should "check their
privilege" at the door. This means white people should consider all
the ways they possess unfair advantages over black people and other
POC. The accusation of white privilege can induce paroxysms of
self-scrutiny and generalized guilt feelings in many white people. All

this is advocated by diversity training guru, Robin DiAngelo, in her bestselling book, *White Fragility*. White guilt can lead to white people kneeling before black people as a sign of contrition, as happened in the madness of 2020 when U.S. House Speaker Nancy Pelosi, Senator Chuck Schumer, and other leftist politicians did exactly that in the Capitol rotunda while wearing Kente cloth stoles provided by the Congressional Black Caucus. When black people and white people kneel together in prayer, that is a good and holy act. When anyone kneels before another mere mortal, that is false worship based on self-hate.

Social situations today in America are usually too complex to divide up precisely how privileges have been apportioned, given personal traits such as race, gender, looks, ability, wealth, and more. Some personal benefits come to us as unearned privileges. Rather than obsess over privilege, it is better to work for a just and fair society in which everyone has the opportunity to advance and where overt prejudice is outlawed (as it largely has been through civil-rights reforms) or frowned upon (through moral awareness). The alternative is for white people to continue to suffer under the weight of endless guilt and for black people to continue to be disempowered because they are deemed unable to help themselves without massive state regulation and top-down control of society. This undermines the agency of black people and induces dependence and ongoing grievance.

To counter the revolutionary fires in the streets and the revolutionary fires in the minds of men and women, we need to overcome apathy. The hour for America is late and the stakes are high. We must not be deceived by the media that is so often used to further a narrative that fails to fit the facts. We need discernment. Rather than being motivated by guilt over America's sins or hopelessly oppressed by them, we need to receive the atonement made for us by Jesus and act as free and good people who care deeply about racial equality and justice.

The rest of this book will try to chart the way.

BURNING IT ALL DOWN?

CHAPTER THREE

WHAT IS AMERICA, AND SHOULD WE BURN IT?

A merica was burning in the summer of 2020, and the fires have not yet been put out. More than a few who took to the streets to protest, and even riot, were and are animated by CRT. Its principles are incompatible with the founding principles and ideals of America. They cannot peacefully coexist with the basic American system of a constitutional republic with democratic representation. CRT has many fellow travelers (such as the violent and anarchistic Antifa)[1] who may not be able to cite CRT authors chapter and verse but who have nonetheless imbibed its essential philosophy and are so motivated.

What is America about? What should Americans think and feel about their country? The United States government was formulated by men well-versed in the philosophy and history of civil government. As American historian Richard Hofstadter wrote:

The Founding Fathers were sages, scientists, men of broad cultivation, many of them apt in classical learning, who used their wide reading in history, politics, and law to solve the exigent problems of their time. No subsequent era in our history has produced so many men of knowledge among its political leaders as the age of John Adams, John Dickinson, Benjamin Franklin, Alexander Hamilton, Thomas Jefferson, James Madison, George Mason, James Wilson, and George Wythe.[2]

That is exceptional, but some tar the whole enterprise as racist and shameful. To settle this matter, we will consider the American creed, American exceptionalism, and our founding documents.

The American Creed

America is as much a set of principles as it is a place. There is a reason why the ill-fated but heroic demonstrators at China's Tiananmen Square in 1989 raised American flags. We will thus speak of the American creed. Americans are not catechized into this creed in the formal manner done by a church (although we need that).[3] However, America has a creed of a certain kind. It has been put in several ways, but essentially states that:

1. America is a republic, affirming that government only legitimately constituted upon "the consent of the governed."
2. America recognizes the potential and weaknesses of human nature, so it does not concentrate power in any single branch of government.
3. America affirms and promotes religious and political freedom, equality, and opportunity.
4. America allows for and encourages upward mobility through individual initiative—the "rags to riches" story

or attaining "the American dream"—not through state action.

5. America is a beacon for the nations, or a "city set on a hill," as Cotton Mather said in a famous sermon. We are a sacred trust between God and "we the people."

6. America endeavors to honor and hold true to its founding documents. Thus, calling something "unconstitutional" is a reproach.

7. America is a place where moral and political reform is possible within the founding ideals and without violence.

8. America is a land that welcomes legal immigrants who want to become Americans and find a better life.

The creed is shaped by our founding documents—the Declaration of Independence and the Constitution—as well as by salient aspects of our history, such as the Revolutionary War (freedom from England), the Civil War (freedom for African Americans), World War II (the victory over fascism), and the Cold War (the victory over Communism).

America as a nation began in 1776, but long before that, settlers came with a mission to the New World—such as those on board the *Mayflower*, which arrived in 1620. Before arriving, most of the male passengers signed the Mayflower Compact, which captures the American spirit of fearing God and wanting

to covenant...into a civil body politic; for our better ordering, and...hereof to enact, constitute, and frame, such just and equal laws, ordinances, acts, constitutions, and offices, from time to time, as shall be thought most meet and convenient for the general good of the colony.[4]

The American creed has freedom or liberty for its backbone, but not license. It is a freedom ordered by law and guided by conscience. It is freedom from tyranny and freedom for virtue. This is a creed to live up to, not an excuse to fail. It allows us to look at America's failings—whether its treatment of Native Americans, African Americans, women, etc.—with neither excuse nor defeatism. It is no accident that in his 1963 "I Have a Dream" speech, Martin Luther King Jr. called for America to "rise up and live out the true meaning of its *creed*: 'We hold these truths to be self-evident, that all men are created equal.'"[5]

While America is not a *Christian* nation by official creed, it has been a God-fearing nation informed by, at its best, a Christian conscience. The American form of civil government is unlike other forms of civil government because it is essentially *covenantal* in its origin and constitution. A *covenant*, in the theological sense, is more than a *contract*. A covenant is made with a sense of honor and obligation before a transcendent reality. It stipulates a binding moral relationship among the people of the covenant who consent to it. A contract, by comparison, is a contingent arrangement made between parties for mutual financial benefit. It is a business transaction, not a sacred trust or moral responsibility.

The Founders articulated a covenant by declaring the United States' moral right, under God, to separate from England and to begin a new nation, which would secure God-given rights through government. Its inspiration was, ironically, the traditions of liberty developed in England over centuries. As Winston Churchill said, "The Declaration of Independence is not only an American document. It follows on the Magna Carta and the Bill of Rights as the third great title-deed in which the liberties of the English-speaking people are founded."[6] It is a republic in that its government is directed by the will of the people according to set principles and procedures, as opposed to any one person or one class of elites controlling the nation. The Declaration of Independence rejected not only the king's right over his colony, but the divine right of kings in favor of a republican government. Consider the majestic Preamble to the Constitution, which is made by "we the people," not by any sovereign.

> We the People of the United States, in Order to form a more perfect Union, establish Justice, insure domestic Tranquility, provide for the common defense, promote the general Welfare, and secure the Blessings of Liberty to ourselves and our Posterity, do ordain and establish this Constitution for the United States of America.

America fought for its freedom from England and declared its distinctive identity in the Declaration (the *why* of America) and later through the Constitution (the *how* of America).[7] Just as the Hebrew republic could fail through disobedience to God, the American republic could be lost through the negligence of its citizens.[8] When Elizabeth Willing Powel asked Benjamin Franklin what the Constitutional Congress of 1787 had given America, he replied to this politically savvy woman, "A Republic, if you can keep it."[9] In a letter dated January 9, 1770, George Washington wrote, "The establishment of our new Government seemed to be the last great experiment, for promoting human happiness, by reasonable compact, in civil Society."[10] It was a well-conceived, though imperfect, experiment—one that could be improved upon or that could fail entirely.

Abraham Lincoln reflected on his place in the meaning of America in light of his reading of a book about George Washington and the Revolutionary War. "I shall be most happy indeed if I shall be an humble instrument in the hands of the Almighty, and of this, *his almost chosen people*, for perpetuating the object of that great struggle."[11]

Consider Lincoln's lapidary phrase—"his almost chosen people." America was not the new Israel, but it was a new nation with a self-reflective creed which began with a Declaration. In 1862, Lincoln sent a message to members of congress encouraging them to prevail in preserving the Union. He said, "We shall nobly save, or meanly lose, the last best hope of earth."[12] The Great Seal of America indicates this sense of call and destiny as well. The first act of Congress after the signing of the Declaration of Independence was to create a Great Seal that would, through image and words, distill the essence of the nation. On it was written *Annuit Coeptis,* which means "undertaking favored by Providence." Below that was written *Novus Ordo Seclorum,* which means "a new order of the ages." America seems exceptional, but is it? We must consult our founding documents, which are so much in dispute today.

Britain abolished slavery in 1807. America lagged beyond it and other nations and only abolished it in 1862,[13] though slavery within it was neither total nor established on principle. That slavery existed at all was a sin; that it was opposed and eventually abolished in America is a victory. How we regard America today depends crucially on how we understand our defining documents: the Declaration of Independence and the Constitution. To them we turn in more detail.

The 1619 Project and Its Riots

Revolution is in the air and revisionism is in the books. The popular rhetoric is that America must be fundamentally transformed because America is fundamentally unsound. The *New York Times* sponsored this view on August 14, 2019, when it released in its *New York Times Magazine* something called the 1619 Project. Its authors, none of whom hold credentials as academic historians, assert (more than argue) that America was racist from the beginning, which dates to the first slaves being brought to America in 1619. This is the true origin of America, they say, and not 1776. They allege that the Revolutionary War was fought to preserve slavery.[14] To say that this is a "minority view" is to grossly overrate it. The project's editor, Nikole Hannah-Jones, quickly won a Pulitzer Prize. A curriculum for the 1619 Project was promptly promoted and used widely.[15]

The 1619 thesis is revisionist history at best and propaganda at worst. It is unsupported by the best scholarship, as was quickly pointed out after its unveiling, and a large body of critique challenges it.[16] The original articles in the project lacked *any documentation*. Specific authors were not identified for any of the major historical articles (although others were.) The head of the project is a journalist who should know well the importance of documenting one's sources; the fact that this was not done is egregious at best and duplicitous at worst.

Given the revisionist and implausible nature of the 1619 Project's claims, these defects are not minor, since the revisionism bears the burden of proof. Peter W. Wood does not overstate the case when, in his detailed criticism, he affirms that "the 1619 Project is, arguably, part of a larger effort to destroy America by people who find our nation unbearably bad."[17] Its master story is that little progress has been made for black people in America, and that the legacy of slavery is evident and prevalent everywhere. It says little about racial progress, but emphasizes past wrongs and their current effects.[18]

This is the new, negative, and desperate narrative of CRT. When the *New York Post* accused the 1619 Project of helping to inspire the protests and riots of the summer of 2020,[19] Hannah-Jones said, "It would be an honor. Thank you."[20] Thus, bad scholarship supported the sabotage of the American system and the summer of brutal and deadly riots.

In November 2021, a book-length version of the 1619 Project was released, this time with documentation, some minor concessions, and new chapters.[21] The theme that *slavery was far worse than typically imagined and that its effects are strongly felt today* remains unchanged. I hope that what follows here will, without engaging all the arguments of the book, present a more measured and well-supported account of the relationship of slavery to the American experience and will offer more hope to transcend whatever residual effects remain.[22]

The Declaration of Independence

Let us begin with the majestic prologue to the Declaration.

> The unanimous Declaration of the thirteen united States of America, When in the Course of human events, it becomes necessary for one people to dissolve the political bands which have connected them with another, and to assume among the powers of the earth, the separate and equal station to which the Laws of Nature and of Nature's God entitle them, a decent respect to the opinions of mankind requires that they should declare the causes which impel them to the separation.
>
> We hold these truths to be self-evident, that all men are created equal, that they are endowed by their Creator with certain unalienable Rights, that among these are Life, Liberty and the pursuit of Happiness.—That to secure these rights, Governments are instituted among Men, deriving their just powers from the consent of the governed...[23]

The Declaration offers to the watching world a philosophy of human rights, civil society, and the state. The Unites States must assume the status due us by "the Laws of Nature and Nature's God," which is an appeal to natural law and to its basis, God Himself. The Declaration affirms that "all men are created equal" with "unalienable rights" that include "life, liberty, and the pursuit of happiness."[24] These rights do not hang on nothing, since they are given by God Himself. The rights endowed by God should be *secured* by governments; governments do not *create* them. "From the principle of equality, the requirement for consent naturally follows: if all men are equal, then none may by right rule another without his consent."[25] Hence, this signaled the end of monarchy and tyranny for America, although it would take a war, as would the end of slavery.

During this time, slavery existed in America, and the principal author of the Declaration, Thomas Jefferson (1743–1826), owned slaves, as did George Washington (who later freed all of them). For some, this invalidates the Declaration, making it fraudulent. But it is not that simple. Not all the states allowed slavery, and abolitionism was in the air at America's founding. Further, the Northwest Ordinance passed in 1787 "to govern the western territories (and passed again by the First Congress and signed into law by President Washington) explicitly bans slavery from those territories and from any states that might be organized there."[26] Furthermore, Jefferson's original draft of the Declaration included a strong condemnation of slavery, which was, alas, removed because of pressure by slaveholding delegates.[27] He was conflicted about slavery and even wrote that because of it, he trembled at the thought that God is just.[28]

A man's ideals may be better than his practice. So, too, for a nation. The Declaration set the tone for the American experiment, raising the bar higher than America had yet reached. But later, pivotal American leaders took the Declaration as a clarion call for freedom for all people, despite the stain of slavery. I will speak of no less than Abraham Lincoln, Frederick Douglass, and Martin Luther King.

President Lincoln harkened back to the Declaration often in his defense of the abolition of slavery. At his Gettysburg Address (November 19, 1863), he said, "Four score and seven years ago our fathers brought forth on this continent, a new nation, conceived in Liberty, and dedicated to the proposition that all men are created equal." Lincoln took this as a justification for the abolition of slavery. He endeavored that "this nation, under God, shall have a new birth of freedom—and that government of the people, by the people, for the people, shall not perish from the earth." Our great president took the Civil War as a sad but necessary continuation of the vision of the Declaration. Historian James Oakes puts this into historical context.

> Lincoln once likened the Declaration to a picture, the Constitution to its frame. For him, as for most antislavery politicians, the men who drafted America's founding charter in the long summer of 1787 had committed the new nation to the principle of fundamental human equality. Fifty years later the great abolitionist William Lloyd Garrison would burn the Constitution in public, vehemently denouncing it as a covenant with Satan, a pro-slavery atrocity. But the majority of abolitionists didn't believe that, no antislavery politician believed that, and neither Abraham Lincoln nor the people who voted for him believed it. For him—for them—the Constitution was an antislavery document.[29]

CRT and BLM advocates affirm the view of the Constitution of William Lloyd Garrison (who was anti-slavery), the Southern slave owners (who were pro-slavery), and John C. Calhoun (1789–1850), the outspoken pro-slavery senator and vice president from South Carolina. As such, they all deem America rotten to the core.

Frederick Douglass (1818–95) likewise had a high view of the Declaration. As a freed slave, he became a masterful orator, abolitionist, writer, and statesman.

> I have said that the Declaration of Independence is the RINGBOLT to the chain of your nation's destiny; so, indeed, I regard it. The principles contained in that instrument are saving principles. Stand by those principles, be true to them on all occasions, in all places, against all foes, and at whatever cost.[30]

Douglass believed in the American experiment and held it accountable to its founding creed of universal rights for "all men." That was ratified when Abraham Lincoln signed The Emancipation Proclamation on January 1, 1863. It read in part:

> By the President of the United States of America:
>   A Proclamation.
>   Whereas, on the twenty-second day of September, in the year of our Lord one thousand eight hundred and sixty-two, a proclamation was issued by the President of the United States, containing, among other things, the following, to wit:
>   "That on the first day of January, in the year of our Lord one thousand eight hundred and sixty-three, all persons held as slaves within any State or designated part of a State, the people whereof shall then be in rebellion against the United States, shall be then, thenceforward,

and forever free; and the Executive Government of the United States, including the military and naval authority thereof, will recognize and maintain the freedom of such persons, and will do no act or acts to repress such persons, or any of them, in any efforts they may make for their actual freedom…"[31]

After the Union forces prevailed over the Confederacy, the 13th, 14th, and 15th Amendments legally inscribed freedom for African Americans. Sadly, Reconstruction stalled and failed. In the South, these blood-bought and battle-born freedoms were breached by segregation, lynching, police brutality, and all the indignities and injustices of Jim Crow.[32] All of that was legally addressed in the Civil Rights reforms.

Martin Luther King Jr.'s "I Have a Dream" speech, delivered in front of the Lincoln Memorial at the nation's capital, harkened back to the Declaration as well. Speaking before a crowd of 250,000, King said:

In a sense we've come to our nation's capital to cash a check. When the architects of our republic wrote the magnificent words of the Constitution and the Declaration of Independence, they were signing a promissory note to which every American was to fall heir. This note was a promise that all men, yes, black men as well as white men, would be guaranteed the "unalienable Rights" of "Life, Liberty and the pursuit of Happiness."

King held America accountable to that "promissory note," which he affirmed was written in "magnificent words." This conviction placed CRT advocates a million miles away from the greatest civil rights leader in American history. King had faith in American principles, despite its terrible racial flaws: "We refuse to believe that there are insufficient funds in the great vaults of opportunity of this nation. And so, we've come to cash this check, a check that will give us upon demand the riches of freedom and the security of justice."[33]

The Constitution and Slavery

In the first quote, Dr. King spoke of "the magnificent words of the Constitution." The courageous and tenacious civil rights activist Fannie Lou Hamer (1917–77) first learned of her constitutional right to vote at a church meeting in Mississippi when she was forty-two years old. Raised dirt-poor and exploited by white people as a sharecropper, she went on to become a major force for black voting rights and the long struggle for equal treatment for her people. She called for America to live up to its ideals, as did Dr. King.[34]

Many tar the Constitution today, claiming that it deems black people as three-fifths human. Few distortions of history are more egregious. This is the clause in question:

> Representatives and direct taxes shall be apportioned among the several states which may be included within this union, according to their respective numbers, which shall be determined by adding to the whole number of free persons, including those bound to service for a term of years, and excluding Indians not taxed, three fifths of all other Persons (Article 1, Section 2).

In other words: count all free persons and indentured servants, do not count Indians, then add three-fifths of the slaves.[35] What does this mean regarding the status of slaves? James Madison in the

Constitutional Convention said that slavery was the crucial problem and "thought it wrong to admit in the Constitution the idea that there could be property in men."[36] The United States Constitution never uses the words "slave" or "race," although the Confederate Constitution (1861) does.[37]

The delegates from the South insisted there could be no constitutional union without the allowance of slavery. Yet, as Robert Goldwin writes, "slavery was a flat contradiction of the principles that are the bedrock foundation of the Constitution—the primacy of the rights of individuals, their equality with respect to their rights, and the consequences that the consent of the governed is the only legitimate source of political power."[38] He states that almost "all the delegates were fully aware that slavery profoundly contradicted these principles and therefore had no proper place in the Constitution."[39]

Since slavery could not be directly undermined in the Constitution without alienating the Southern states, the anti-slavery delegates wanted to make "the political base for slavery as weak as possible, to diminish its influence and improve the chances of eradicating it sometime in the future."[40] Thus, the Constitution was a compromise between the pro-slavery Southern states and the anti-slavery Northern states. The Northerners feared that the Southern states would break off into their own nation without a compromise, so a deal was struck. The Southern delegates wanted their slaves' numbers counted as part of the population in order to increase their representation in Congress and gain more power over the North.

The three-fifths compromise had nothing to do with slaves being viewed as three-fifths human; rather, *it allowed the Northern delegates to limit the political power of the South, who would not let their slaves vote anyway.* The anti-slavery delegates would not want these non-voting slaves to count at all, since it gave the South more political power, but a compromise was needed. As Golding notes, "If all the slaves had been included, as the Southerners wanted, the slave states would have had 50 percent of the seats [in Congress]. But agreeing to three-fifths, the slave states ended up with 47 percent—not negligible, but still a minority likely to be outvoted on slavery issues."[41] The three-fifths clause weakened the power of the pro-slavery South; it was a ticking time bomb for black freedom that eventually detonated against slavery.

However, one section of the Constitution (Article IV, Section 2, Paragraph 3), which came to be known as "the fugitive slave clause," was interpreted to oblige free states to return runaways to Southern states. As Paul Johnson notes, this "caused more hatred, anger, and venom on both sides of the slave line than any other issue and was a prime cause of the eventual conflict."[42]

Frederick Douglass at first thought the Constitution was pro-slavery.[43] However, he changed his mind and defended it. His premier biographer, David Blight, writes that Douglass "was a serious constitutional thinker, and few Americans have ever analyzed race with more poignancy and nuance than this mostly self-taught genius with words."[44]

Douglass observed that the Constitution's allowance of the slave trade (Article 1, Section 9, Clause 1) to extend twenty years from the Constitution's ratification was meant to cut off the supply and so, eventually, stop the practice. As he said, "The American statesmen, in providing for the abolition of the slave trade, thought they were providing for the abolition of the slavery."[45] Further, this provision "says to the slave States, the price you will have to pay for coming into the American Union is, that the slave trade, which you would carry on indefinitely out of the Union, shall be put an end to in twenty years if you come into the Union."[46]

The Constitution Today

Those who try to fathom (1) the proper interpretation of the Declaration, (2) the Declaration's relationship to the Constitution, and (3) the Constitution itself find themselves in deep waters—not impossible to navigate, but difficult and choppy, and requiring astute scholarship. Still, we can confidently rule out the 1619 Project's revisionism. My view is that the "declaration was the conscience of the constitution"[47] and that the "the antislavery Constitution" is the real Constitution.[48] That was the vision of Abraham Lincoln, Frederick Douglass, and Martin Luther King Jr. Even if my view is incorrect, the positive understanding of "all men are created equal" with "inalienable rights" has been incorporated into the American creed in God's Providence. Even on a more negative reading of the Declaration and the Constitution (as promulgated by CRT), these documents became the eventual inspiration for a fairer, freer, and more just society. I, for one, am not about to abolish them because of their flaws. Shelby Steele concludes his brilliant book, *Shame*, with these words: "America's essential truth—the deepest theme of our identity—is still freedom. Freedom is still our mother tongue."[49] In light of our founding documents and American history, what kind of allegiance do we, as a free and responsible people, owe our country?

American Patriotism

A qualified patriotism is in order for the common good, given the good of the American Creed and in the providence of God. The Lord placed us where we are for a reason: as actors who shape history (Acts 17:26–27). We live in nations, but the nation is a poor excuse for the church, since it alone has received the promise of Jesus Christ that "the gates of hell will not prevail against it" (Matthew 16:18). No nation is eternally secure before a holy God (Isaiah 40:15–17), but seeking the welfare of one's country and appreciating its unique benefits is the measure of wisdom (Jeremiah 29:1–7; Matthew 5:16–18). That is what I mean by "qualified patriotism."

The notion of "My country, right or wrong" is wrong. A patriot in this sense thinks their nation has a messianic role in world history. However, to recognize that America has a unique and salutary role in the world, given its natural resources, beauty, history, and creed, need not be idolatrous. The American system lays a strong foundation for preserving liberty, ensuring basic rights, and allowing for constructive change in national life. Appreciation for America as a nation and a commitment to American ideals is commendable. (I will speak of appropriate "civil rituals" in our final chapter.)

American Nationalism

Love of country becomes noxious, unbiblical, and even un-American when it exalts America above the moral law; when it ignores, excuses, or glosses over America's faults; and when it exempts America from the scrutiny of "the laws of nature and nature's God." If nationalism becomes an instinctive and unreflective *nativism*, it becomes noxious. Nativism is usually associated with anti-Catholic sentiment and politics in the 1920s in America when Catholic immigrants (usually Italian) were unwelcomed by *native* Americans (not Indians). Nativism means hostility to immigrants based on their ethnicity or religion.

Nationalism's toxicity increases when it deems any political leader as exempt from any moral scrutiny. God did not except the kings of Israel from His standards (Deuteronomy 17:14–20), and neither should we. Or, as the Psalmist asks, "Can wicked rulers be allied with you, those who frame injustice by statute?" (Psalm 94:20).

White Nationalism

What black political scientist Carol Swain calls "white nationalism" is a response to racial tensions due to political and demographic change in the United States.[50] Unlike older groups such as the Ku Klux Klan or the American Nazi Party, white nationalists tend to be younger and more articulate in their grievances. They feel threatened by affirmative action programs that disadvantage them as white citizens. They are likewise concerned about the flood of immigrants—legal and illegal, but mostly illegal—who may compete with them for jobs or who tend to undermine the American identity. They feel disadvantaged because they are white and want equal standing with POC. White nationalists in this sense are not necessarily racist, xenophobic, or part of the Alt-Right (for which I have no sympathy). Rather, they are concerned about their rights and opportunities as American citizens who feel marginalized or left behind.

This feeling of being marginalized because of being white was captured in a tweet by the celebrated black "antiracist," Ibram X. Kendi:

> More than a third of White students lied about their race on college applications, and about half of these applicants lied about being Native American. More than three-fourths of these students who lied about their race were accepted.[51]

This tweet (which Kendi quickly deleted) was linked to an article in *The Hill*, which cited a study by *Intelligent* which reported that in a poll of 1,250 white people ages sixteen and older, "34% of white Americans who applied to colleges or universities admit to lying about being a racial minority on their application."[52] This deception is wrong, but it is understandable given the kind of preferences made for POC in college admissions.

Kendi posted the tweet to point out the perfidy of white people, but then deleted it—presumably because it shows that these white people thought they would be *better off* if they posed as POC and not white. So much for white privilege there. This does not fit Kendi's narrative of systemic racism, so it was deleted. The admissions situation contradicts a typical CRT statement found at the African American Museum of History and Culture: "Being white does not mean you have not faced hardships or oppression based on the color of your skin."[53]

The American creed and our nation's attempts to live up to it prove its exceptionalism.[54] However, that grants America no exemption from moral scrutiny or the righteous judgments of Providence. As Jesus said, "To whom much is given, much is required" (Luke 12:48). Much has been given to America, and God requires much of her. Although this quote cannot be attributed to Alexis de Tocqueville (as it often is),[55] it is, nonetheless, a fitting conclusion, because it is true: "America is great because she is good, and if America ever ceases to be good, she will cease to be great."

CHAPTER FOUR

AMERICA AND SYSTEMIC RACISM

In light of America's founding documents, we can rule out the CRT and 1619 allegations that America is racist in its origin, and so must be racist if it lives true to its origin. On the contrary, the more America lives up to its creed, the less racist it will be. Nevertheless, many claim that America now (however we interpret its origin) is "systemically racist" and thus needs systemic change of a radical sort.

Baked into the System?

Unfairness to black people and other POC is taken to be "baked into the system" and goes beyond racist attitudes and actions by individuals. Interestingly, when something is "baked in," that means it cannot be "baked out"; the only remedy is to burn it to a crisp and start over with a new recipe. Thus, racial disparities in achievement are due to racism. Thus, if disparities exist and have not been eliminated through the American system as it is, then a strong dose of "antiracism" is needed. For Ibram X. Kendi, this means abolishing capitalism and bringing in other systemic reforms. Kendi is clear and forceful in this program.

> The only remedy to racist discrimination is antiracist discrimination. The only remedy to past discrimination is present discrimination. The only remedy to present discrimination is future discrimination.[1]

This chapter will challenge Kendi's ungrounded assumption that disparities in achievement or benefits between blacks and whites are always the result of racism and thus require reverse discrimination to counteract it. It will also challenge his rejection of equality under law and of meritocracy.[2] But in light of his thesis, Kendi proposed an "Anti-Racist Amendment to the Constitution" to "fix the original sin of racism." It would be guided by two "anti-racist principals: Racial inequity is evidence of racist policy and the different racial groups are equals."[3] Of course "different racial groups are equals," but to assume that "inequity" is, by itself, "evidence of racist policy" is implausible in the extreme, as we will note. Moreover, Kendi's setup would empower the state to overrule financial, economic, and personal factors that contribute to nonproportional representation at the expense of personal liberties. For now, a quote from Thomas Sowell is enough to clear the air:

> The conclusion of French historian Fernand Braudel—that "In no society have all regions and all parts of the population developed equally"—is a conclusion reached by many others who have done empirical studies of peoples, institutions and societies around the world. A landmark international study

of ethnic groups by Professor Donald L. Horowitz of Duke University concluded that the idea of "proportional representation" of such groups was something that "few, if any, societies have ever approximated."[4]

We will take up capitalism in a later chapter, but the widespread claim that disparities in achievements by race must be explained by racism and can only be addressed by "equity" (equal outcomes enforced by law) needs to be challenged.

"Systemic racism" may have first been used by Black Panther Stokely Carmichael in the 1960s as part of the "black power" ideology, which pitted itself against the nonviolent and reformist approach of Martin Luther King Jr. and his cohorts, such as John Lewis.[5] Earlier, the term "institutional racism" was used instead of "systemic racism." David Horowitz's comments are on target:

> The very phrase "institutional racism" is, of course, of leftist provenance. Like "ruling class" it refers to an abstraction. It is a totalitarian term. It does not specify particular, accountable individuals. You are a class enemy (or, in this case, a race enemy) not because of anything you actually think or do, but "objectively"—because you are situated in a structure of power that provides you (white skin) privilege.[6]

"Systemic racism" is a term bandied about constantly and used to explain negative outcomes for black people. But it is usually invoked with little clarity as to its meaning or how it could be verified or falsified. Let us try to clarify. Then we will make judgments. First let us consider the term *racism*, then *systemic*.

What Is Racism?

Racism is a vicious attitude, and a racist is a bad person. Historically, racism has referred to individuals who hold disparaging beliefs and negative emotions about members of races outside of their own. A racist discriminates wrongly and on the basis of race. Discrimination, in this sense, is based on prejudice, which is an unfair evaluation based on irrelevant characteristics, such as race.

On this account, one could be condemned as a racist or exonerated from the charge based on his or her beliefs, emotions, and actions. But CRT extends the meaning of racism to systems independent of these criteria. This is a main claim of *White Fragility* by Robin DiAngelo, along with the idea that all white people are racist. If a white person denies this, it only proves that they are covering it up. So, there is no escape.[7] There is no doubt that the Jim Crow South, for example, was racist *as a system*, given its laws and culture, but the question is whether the United States is systemically racist today.

CRT advocates generally claim that only white people can be racist. POC cannot be racist, since they are an oppressed group. This ideological rendering of the term "racism" is foreign to the origin and traditional meaning of the word. If racism means "unfair prejudice against someone simply because he or she belongs to another race," then racism pertains to anyone of any race who demonstrates that quality. (An exception to this is Ibram X. Kendi, who thinks that POC can be racist, that he himself has been racist, and sometimes still is a racist.[8] We will address the more common view.)

If only those members of the oppressing race can be racist, then racism is actually not about race essentially, but about contingent power relations between racial groups. Historically, racism concerns wrongful attitudes about race, not necessarily about disparities of power. But on CRT grounds, if black people were the ruling class and dominated white people, then all black people would be racists against all white people, and white people could never be racists against black people. Racism then becomes contingent on power dynamics, and race, ironically, is not the central determining factor.

But perhaps CRT thinkers are racial essentialists after all: To be white is to be oppressive and racist, they say. If so, then to be non-white means you are off the hook concerning vicious racial views and acts. If so, the human race is necessarily and inexorably bifurcated and balkanized by race—neither a happy thought nor a true one.

CRT teaches that racism is so insinuated into the system and into the soul that "microaggressions" against POC and women are common. Columbia University Professor Derald Wing Sue defines microaggressions as "brief, everyday exchanges that send denigrating messages to certain individuals because of their group membership."[9] Yes, we may snub each other in subtle and nonviolent ways. That is an offense against love. Some of this disrespect is racially based, to be sure.

Nevertheless, a fixation on looking for offense and interpreting statements or gestures in the worst light can be peevish and sow unnecessary discord and suspicion. For some steeped in CRT, the very accusation of racism is enough to convict the accused without trial and without appeal.[10] Much of this thinking is rooted in Michel Foucault's philosophy of power relations, which claims that every action is the exercise of power.[11] Thus, anything the oppressor group says can be taken as an attempt to exercise racist power over POC who, in turn, take offense, demand an apology or reparations—or worse yet, demand cancellation. The answer to this chronic suspicion is to speak carefully and listen carefully, always addressing the speaker's intent. We need to control our tongue and even our body language in order to respect others (James 3:1–12).

Whiteness

On the CRT account of racism, white people need to be less white or to renounce their "whiteness." The African American History Museum says this about it:

> Whiteness (and its accepted normality) also exists as everyday microaggressions toward people of color. Acts of microaggressions include verbal, nonverbal, and environmental slights, snubs or insults toward nonwhites. Whether intentional or not, these attitudes communicate hostile, derogatory, or harmful messages.[12]

If that is what being white means, then one should be less white. But that is not what "being white" means; that is what *some* white people *do*. To universalize "whiteness" as "racist" is unfair and racist in itself.

What about "white privilege"? The African American History Museum web page gives this definition:

> Since white people in America hold most of the political, institutional, and economic power, they receive advantages that nonwhite groups do not. These benefits and advantages, of varying degrees, are known as white privilege.[13]

On this view, racism is perpetuated by white people experiencing benefits simply because of their white skin that those with more pigmentation do not receive. That is debatable as a general principle of analysis, since so many white people are far from any political, institutional, or economic power. Consider the chronically and intergenerationally poor in Appalachia.[14] Further, nonwhite groups in America do receive, in some cases, "advantages" that white people do not, such as affirmative action. This makes race a determining factor in hiring for jobs and for admission into colleges.

Disparities and Racism

But what of economic disparities between races today? The group earning the highest median annual income in America is not white people, but Asians. Leading the pack of Asians are those from India at $119,000 per year.[15] Here are median household incomes by race in the United States as of 2020, according to Statistica: Asian $94,903; white $74,912; Hispanic $55,312; black $45,870.[16] Should we attribute these differences solely or mainly to racism?

Racism, as an individual fault, still exists in America. There are racist organizations as well, such as the American Nazi Party, the Ku Klux Klan,[17] and some alt-right groups.[18] But is the whole system racist today? We should remember that disparities in achievement (on multiple indices) have multiple causes. The CRT account is one of racial reductionism, and like all reductionisms, it misses the bigger picture given its conceptual myopia. Sowell summarizes hundreds of pages of research in this statement:

> The bedrock assumption underlying many political or ideological crusades is that socioeconomic disparities are automatically somebody's fault, so that our choices are either to blame society or to "blame the victim." Yet whose fault are demographic differences, geographic differences, birth order differences or cultural differences that evolved over the centuries before any of us were born?
>
> If we are serious about seeking causation, we must look beyond emotional words, which are not necessarily intended to inform or convince, but often achieve their goal

if they simply overwhelm through repetition or silence through intimidation.[19]

Throughout his career, Sowell has looked at cultural factors regarding disparate outcomes among races in countries around the world. While he—a black man born in 1930—knows well that racism still exists in America and elsewhere, that need not retard social progress nor be viewed as the decisive factor in differential outcomes by race. It never stopped him. Along those lines, consider some key elements of disparities between black people and other groups.

Underachievement and Disparities

Before becoming president, Barack Obama—neither a conservative nor a friend of the free market—exposed a raw wound of black underachievement that is hardly the fault of the free market and which socialism will not heal: the absence of fathers in the contemporary black family. I quote his Father's Day remarks at the Apostolic Church of God in Chicago on June 15, 2008, at some length.

> Of all the rocks upon which we build our lives, we are reminded today that family is the most important. And we are called to recognize and honor how critical every father is to that foundation. They are teachers and coaches. They are mentors and role models. They are examples of success and the men who constantly push us toward it.
>
> But if we are honest with ourselves, we'll admit that what too many fathers also are is missing—missing from too many lives and too many homes. They have abandoned their responsibilities, acting like boys instead of men. And the foundations of our families are weaker because of it.

You and I know how true this is in the African-American community. We know that more than half of all black children live in single-parent households, a number that has doubled—doubled—since we were children. We know the statistics—that children who grow up without a father are five times more likely to live in poverty and commit crime; nine times more likely to drop out of schools and twenty times more likely to end up in prison. They are more likely to have behavioral problems, or run away from home, or become teenage parents themselves. And the foundations of our community are weaker because of it.[20]

Obama was right that (1) the family is the most important social institution (not the state), (2) fathers are essential for strong families (as are mothers) (3) too many fathers are missing from families, and that (4) the lack of fathers adversely affects the black community in terms of crime, incarceration, teenage parentage, and educational failure.[21] More recent statistics back up these sad observations.[22] Writing for the Department of Labor in 1965, Daniel Patrick Moynihan's report, *The Negro Family: A Case for National Action*, warned that the rising illegitimacy rate among black families was a dangerous trend that threatened the well-being of black people in America. He was mostly but sadly right, although he received much criticism and was even tarred as a racist.

The distresses of America's black community have many causes, but none now seem *primarily* economic, such that government programs are the cure; they are, rather, cultural and rooted in moral values and habits.[23] One can endlessly blame "the legacy of slavery," but we should consider the "legacy of liberalism," as Thomas Sowell does. This long passage summarizes much of Sowell's work developed thoroughly in his many books:

If we wanted to be serious about evidence, we might compare where blacks stood a hundred years after the end of slavery with where they stood after thirty years of the liberal welfare state....

Despite the grand myth that black economic progress began or accelerated with the passage of the civil rights laws and "war on poverty" programs of the 1960s, the cold fact is that the poverty rate among blacks fell from 87 percent in 1940 to 47 percent by 1960. This was before any of those programs began.

Over the next twenty years, the poverty rate among blacks fell another 18 percentage points, compared to the forty-point drop in the previous twenty years. This was the continuation of a previous economic trend, at a slower rate of progress, not the economic grand deliverance proclaimed by liberals and self-serving black "leaders."

Ending the Jim Crow laws was a landmark achievement. But, despite the great proliferation of black political and other "leaders" that resulted from the laws and policies of the 1960s, nothing comparable happened economically. And there were serious retrogressions socially.

Nearly a hundred years of the supposed "legacy of slavery" found most black children being raised in two-parent families in 1960. But thirty years after the liberal welfare state found the great majority of black children being raised by a single parent.

The murder rate among blacks in 1960 was one-half of what it became twenty years later, after a legacy of liberals' law enforcement policies. Public housing projects in the first half of the twentieth century were clean, safe places, where people slept outside on hot summer nights, when they were too poor to afford air conditioning. That was before admissions standards for public housing projects were lowered or abandoned, in the euphoria of liberal non-judgmental notions. And it was before the toxic message of victimhood was spread by liberals. We all know what hell holes public housing has become in our times.[24]

Sowell has frequently documented the ill effects of deeming the state as the best answer to black poverty or other social malaise. He has repeatedly argued that *cultural values* play a more significant role in economic and educational outcomes than other factors.[25] For example, some ethnic groups thrive economically even in situations where they are disliked and discriminated against. "Both in Canada and the United States, the Japanese have significantly higher incomes than white people, who have a documented history of severe anti-Japanese discrimination in both countries."[26] The same applies broadly to the overseas Chinese, who, though they are often disliked by their adopted countries, advance economically and culturally.[27]

The idea that the legacy of slavery, Jim Crow, redlining, and present conditions hamstring POC undermines the agency of disadvantaged POC. Shelby Steele has long insisted that as long as black people make their freedom and achievement dependent on state interventions, they will languish in resentment and underachievement.[28] CRT finds ever more layers of oppression foisted on black people by white people, and it thus stokes the fires of resentment and discontent in black people, who are then forever beholden on the white oppressors to free them. Consider an illustration from the cover of Miles Davis's recording, "On the Corner" (1972). A hipper-than-hip black man sports a button that says, "Free me." Ever since I first saw that as a teenager, it struck me as off base, putting the agency for freedom in the wrong place.

Kendi encapsulates this idea, writing, "To be antiracist is to say the political and economic conditions, not the people, in poor Black neighborhoods are pathological."[29] So, for Kendi, to identify behaviors of individuals as "pathological" is not antiracist, which means it is racist. But this is a false dichotomy. Both the conditions and behaviors are pathological and we should never reduce people to their conditions, since that undermines human agency and responsibility.

Our language often betrays how we think of groups of people, especially when we attribute causation to impersonal forces beyond human control. As Sowell notes: "Many of the words and phrases used in the media and among academics suggest that things simply happen to people, rather than being caused by their own choices or behavior."[30] We hear of an "epidemic" of drug use or teenage pregnancy, as if these were caught like the cold or the flu. There are "forces that drive people to commit crimes."[31] "Implicit in much of this verbiage is the notion that the rules were rigged for or against some individual or group. But whether, or to what extent, this is true is precisely the issue that should be argued—not circumvented by verbal sleight-of-hand."[32] Or we hear that "society" denies "access to health care" or "access to affordable housing" when the issue concerns individual actors who chose to spend or make their money in particular ways and in particular circumstances. "Systemic racism" is used to explain all manner of ills for POC, often sweeping under the sociological rug the personal responsibility of those involved. But this factor is crucial. There is

> voluminous evidence from countries around the world
> [that] repeatedly shows particular immigrant groups begin-
> ning their lives destitute in a new country, taking low-level
> jobs disdained by the native population, and yet ultimately
> rising above the economic level of those around them. The
> "overseas Chinese" have done this throughout Southeast

Asia and in several Western Hemisphere nations. Jews have done the same in numerous countries. The history of the United States has seen this achievement repeated by a number of European immigrant groups and by the Japanese and the Cubans, among others.[33]

But the modern welfare state denies or minimizes these personal factors, tramples on human values and agency, and substitutes impersonal programs.

Any number of factors lead to non-proportional representation in various professions and achievements in a society. Racism is one of them, but not necessarily determinative. Consider the average age of an ethnic group correlated with average income. The median (or average) age of Hispanics in America is twenty-seven, while the average age of Japanese is fifty-one. The median age of blacks in America is thirty-four. The median age for whites is forty-four.[34] Given our economy, being considerably older means one makes more money than someone who is considerably younger, since the older person typically has more education, has built-up job experience, has made investments, and so on. Another factor is geographic.[35] Sowell notes that people who live in mountainous regions (of whatever ethnicity and in any country) suffer social disadvantages in relation to those who do not live in such areas. This is because of the difficulties in transportation and isolation. Consider those who live in the Appalachian region of the United States—known as "hillbillies"—that is dogged by poverty, substance abuse, and welfare dependency. It is largely white.

However, the power of culture means that racism may be countered successfully by individual and family values. These include keeping nuclear families intact, exercising self-control (i.e., avoiding addictions) and delayed gratification, shunning criminality, retaining employment, keeping a future orientation, and pursuing education.

Help through the State?

The transforming power of state intervention was the premise of the Great Society federal programs which President John F. Kennedy began but which President Lyndon Johnson dramatically brought into being. The underlying belief was that pathological conditions could be cured by wealth transfers; thus Johnson declared "war on poverty."[36] Their hubris was thinking that if the United States could win World War II, it could surely win a war on poverty with enough money and social scientists. Charles Murray notes the magnitude of the change: "Overall, civilian welfare costs increased by twenty times from 1950–1980, in constant dollars. During the same period, the United States population increased by half."[37]

But the mammoth top-down, bureaucratic programs often had the unintended consequence (or side effect) of disempowering POC, who became dependent on the state rather than more equipped to flourish as productive citizens. The effect on black families has been severe; welfare programs supported unmarried mothers, and in too many cases, that had the unintended consequence of rewarding illegitimacy. Paradoxically, massive state interventions for POC seem to hurt more than help.[38] The past should be a prologue for resisting even more statist interventions in the name of "equity."[39] This can be summarized by the title of Jason Riley's convincing and well-researched book, *Please Stop Helping Us: How Liberals Make It Harder for Blacks to Succeed.*[40]

Even if governmental policies are wholly or partially to blame for the present disparities between white and black people, it does not follow that the civil government is the vehicle to rectify or ameliorate these wrongs. Legal scholar Amy Wax illustrates this with "The Parable of the Pedestrian": A woman is hit by a reckless driver, severely injuring her spine. The injury takes years of painstaking physical therapy to improve. Although she was the victim, she has the responsibility to rehabilitate herself—even if the driver pays all her medical bills and a large fine. He cannot do the physical therapy for her. But the victim could give up and write a memoir on the injustice of the accident and the evils of the driver. When her therapists make her work harder, she can say they are "blaming the victim." However, "the nature of her injury precludes the possibility of anyone besides her healing it." In the same way, disadvantaged POC may have been hurt by "the system," but the system may not be of much or any help in their betterment.[41]

Derrick Bell and the Permanence of Racism

I reviewed Derrick Bell's ideas briefly in a previous chapter, but now need to address his claims about systemic racism. Bell charges that the supposed gains for black people in the Civil Rights era were chimeras and that racism is "permanent" in America.[42] If black people have made any racial progress, it is because of "interest convergence"— his theory that white people will only cede power or grant privileges to black people if it is in their own interest to do so. White people have not been genuinely altruistic toward black people, he claims, although it may appear so. Bell writes: "Black rights are recognized and protected when and only so long as policymakers perceive that such advances will further interests that are their primary concern."[43]

By "policymakers," Bell refers to the white establishment, and by "interests" he means the interests of that establishment. He denies that the policymakers could legitimately be concerned with "black rights" for their own sake. Given human selfishness and the realities of racism, this sometimes occurs. However, to claim it as a controlling principle is debatable and demands proof.

Bell wanted to expand the resources on the treatment of black people in America by appealing to testimonial evidence, narratives, and even fiction. His book, *Faces at the Bottom of the Well*, is mostly made up of stories and dialogues about race. In his well-known story "The Space Traders," aliens come to earth with a bargain: they will solve the nation's pollution and debt crisis (caused by conservative policies) if the United States will surrender all black people to them to be taken off the planet. The aliens vouchsafe nothing about the fate of the black people. The federal government puts it to a vote, and the space traders' deal is accepted 70 percent to 30 percent.[44]

Bell uses this scenario to explore multiple themes in politics and race relations, which makes for interesting reading. Still, the idea is absurd. I would never consider it, nor can I imagine any of my friends or colleagues would consider it. Perhaps Bell does not believe it either, but uses it as a fantastical image for racist realities. However, in the foreword to a new edition of *Faces at the Bottom of the Well*, Michelle Alexander, author of *The New Jim Crow*, says, "I do not recall discussing this story with any person—not one—who doubted things would go down precisely that way in real life. None of us questioned the outcome."[45] This is not a scientific sampling, but it is troubling indeed.

Bell claims that white interest in black well-being is strictly self-interested and utilitarian. Make the right deal, and the dominant culture will even bid black people farewell, sending them off into unknown space never to return. How many Americans in 1992 would have agreed with that, and how many now? The answer in both cases is this: only the most egregious racists.

Bell's "interest convergence thesis" may apply to some people, given human turpitude. However, counterexamples to it abound, such as the 700,000 white Union soldiers who died fighting against slavery in the Civil War; the white "freedom riders," who at their own peril accompanied black people on buses in the South in 1961 to protest segregation in public transportation; and the 60,000 white people (out of 250,000 total) who flocked to the National Mall to hear Martin Luther King Jr.'s "I Have A Dream" speech in Washington,

D.C., in 1963. One could go on, of course. Thus, the interest convergence principle is overly pessimistic at best, and cynical and defeatist at worst. As a universal or even a general principle, it is simply false.

We cannot take up the wide array of other claims made by Bell, who wrote influential articles and books over several decades, but three more of them merit scrutiny. First, that black people's "lived experience" must count in assessing the state of their condition; second, that black people have made few gains since the Civil Rights era; and third, that racism is permanent in America.

The emphasis on "lived experience" is part of "standpoint theory" and grows out of postmodernist philosophy. Postmodernism claimed that there is no such thing as: (1) objective truth, (2) objective rationality, or (3) epistemic neutrality (i.e., everyone is biased).[46] However, when wedded to critical legal theory, postmodernism morphs into standpoint epistemology. To this is added the idea that (4) oppressed minorities have a singularly privileged perspective on reality, given their oppression. This is as close to objective truth as it gets, so their view must be accepted and their proposals heeded.

On this view, epistemology is a matter of social justice in which the oppressed set the terms of the debate. Whereas postmodernism dissolves truth into relative perspectives and warns of totalizing metanarratives (such as religion and Marxism), standpoint epistemology brings back a totalizing narrative—but this time, it is the narrative of the oppressed, who uniquely and infallibly know the score. POC are those who have lost the social battles and can find power by claiming victimhood and the unique insights into reality that it affords. Is this credible?

There is no reason why supposed victims should have a monopoly on defining reality. Yes, they have a unique perspective, and one worth heeding. But there is no reason to privilege that perspective among all others. In order to determine the truth, one needs evidence and logic, neither of which concern social standing—as oppressor or as oppressed. "Lived experience" is unique to the person who lives it, and every person experiences the world differently. Making this appeal will not rationally ground the CRT perspective, since lived experiences differ. Black historian and student of race in America, Shelby Steele, writes from his lived experience. Raised by a black father and white mother who were activists for the civil rights vision, he later embraced leftist black radicalism in the 1960s and 70s before becoming disenchanted with it and returned to Martin Luther King's colorblind ethic. As he said in an interview in 2006, "I show you how these thoughts and feelings and ideas evolve out of my experience because I want to communicate with people on that level: as human beings."[47] Yet Steele wisely never defaults to his "lived experience" alone to make his arguments. When "my truth" means that nothing can refute, qualify, or add to that perspective, then we have left reason and evidence behind. As Thomas Chatterton Williams put it in critiquing Ta-Nehisi Coates:

> Such logic extends a disturbing trend in left-of-center public thinking: identity epistemology, or knowing-through-being, somewhere along the line became identity ethics, or morality-through-being. Accordingly, whiteness and wrongness have become interchangeable—the high ground is now accessible only by way of "allyship," which is to say silence and total repentance. The upside to this new white burden, of course, is that whichever way they may choose, those deemed white remain this nation's primary actors.[48]

"Knowing-through-being" epistemology does not level the playing field of discourse. It begs questions and issues unfair demands that inhibit rational debate.

Second, the cumulative effects of the Civil Rights movement is a complicated subject, but suffice to say that they were an advance for POC in fundamental legal rights. But positive social change needs more than mere change in laws, and this is where CRT advocates and conservatives disagree. Massive state programs are not the answer for nagging problems with POC, especially anything like the proposed "Anti-Racism Amendment" to the Constitution. The Great Society reforms, on balance, were a setback for most POC, especially black people, as Sowell argued above.

Third, Bell's claim that American racism is permanent means that all white Americans are permanently racist and immune to reform. If that is true, then white people are inferior to black people in their essence. They are, thus, racists-in-being who can't help but foster systemically racist societies. This construction, along with Bell's improbable interest convergence thesis, erects a permanent antagonism between white and black people.[49] This is a counsel of despair; and it is equally untrue concerning the racial progress made in America and the American promise that motivated black people such as Frederick Douglass, Fanny Lou Hamer, John Lewis, and Martin Luther King to act as they did.

Affirmative Action on Trial

For some, affirmative action is a closed case: it is good and it helps black people. Nevertheless, the case is not closed, and the American creed should cause us to question it.

After the Civil Rights victories of the 1960s, Lyndon Johnson and others argued for what they called "affirmative action." This meant that African Americans would be given every opportunity to fairly compete with those of other races in American society. To that end, several educational and social programs were launched in what was called the Great Society. At that time, affirmative action did not entail quotas in employment or education for black people, which meant discrimination against equally or greater-skilled members of other races. This original understanding can be called "equal opportunity." President John F. Kennedy's Executive Order No. 10,925 in 1961 said "that federal contractors" should "take affirmative action to ensure that the applicants are employed, and that employees are treated during employment, without regard to their race, creed, color, or national origin."[50] But the meaning of "affirmative action" would radically change—even into its opposite.

Most Democrats, union leaders, and civil rights leaders in the late 1960s and early 1970s opposed this new kind of affirmative action because it would disadvantage competent white people (and others) and generate resentment between the races. For example, Democrat Hubert Humphrey, who ran for president in 1968, opposed it. While guiding the 1964 Civil Rights Bill through the U.S. Senate, he assured his colleagues that it "does not require an employer to achieve any kind of racial balance in his work force by giving preferential treatment to any individual or group."[51]

The constitutional argument is that affirmative action violates the equal protection clause of the Fifteenth Amendment, which in part reads:

> No State shall make or enforce any law which shall abridge the privileges or immunities of citizens of the United States; nor shall any State deprive any person of life, liberty, or property, without due process of law; nor deny to any person within its jurisdiction the equal protection of the laws.

However, President Richard Nixon (1913–94) unilaterally instituted affirmative action in 1969, and it has been in place ever since throughout business and education.[52] The equal-opportunity legislation articulated by Kennedy and Humphrey worked against racial discrimination. However, the argument against affirmative action as it is now conceived is two-fold—the in-principle argument and the in-practice argument.

The in-principle argument was just explained, but let me expand the discussion. Individuals, of whatever race, should be hired for jobs or admitted to educational institutions on the basis of merit, not because of group membership. No one should be discriminated against because of race; nor should anyone be favored on the basis of race. This is the classic idea of creating a level playing field—or a *fairly level* playing field, since perfection is not possible among fallen mortals. And when civil governments try to implement perfection through legislation, this always backfires through deleterious unintended consequences.

This stance squarely fits the Fifteenth Amendment. This concept was adopted in 1996 in the state of California in Proposition 209, which added the following language to the state's constitution: "The state shall not discriminate against, or grant preferential treatment to, any individual or group on the basis of race, sex, color, ethnicity, or national origin." It is still in effect.

Competence can be penalized through affirmative action. This is painfully evident in admission policies at high schools, colleges, and universities. For decades, many schools have stratified standards for admissions by race. Asians must pass the highest standards for admission. The reasoning is that their excellent academic ratings are due to unearned and unfair "privilege," even though high-achieving Asian Americans have faced race-related discrimination and resentment, especially in college and even high school admissions.

Kenny Xu has written a ringing defense of a colorblind, level-playing-field approach in *An Inconvenient Minority: The Attack on*

Asian American Excellence and the Fight for Meritocracy.[53] Asian
Americans are not receiving fair treatment. For example, Thomas
Jefferson High School for Math and Science in Arlington, Virginia,
was for many years one of the best schools in the region. Starting in
the 2000s, increasing numbers of Asian Americans were admitted.
This merit-based enrollment meant that by 2020, 72 percent of its
students were Asian-American. This is simply due to the cultural
values of hard work and studiousness in Asian American families.
However, after the death of George Floyd and "the racial reckoning"
of 2020, the school was deemed racist because Asian Americans do
not make up 72 percent of the general population and because in
2020, only six black students were admitted. The school used stan-
dardized test scores and no quotas to determine who got in. The
school board pressured the school to change, and antiracist impresario
Ibram X. Kendi was brought in for a fee of $20,000 to awaken them
all to the racism inherent in non-proportional representation.[54]

This merit-based, outstanding school then switched to a system
where one hundred of its 480 spots became purely merit-based, but
"the rest would go to any students about a 3.5 GPA, with the required
courses, by the luck of the draw."[55] This was done to "increase diversity," colorblind merit be damned. It is no surprise that Xu wrote his
book to protest this kind of thoughtless prejudice, which is widespread
in the United States. Identity politics in this nation ironically undermines the unique, individual identities based on people's abilities and
potential, and subsumes them under group association.[56]

The practical argument against affirmative action is that while it
has helped some POC over the years, its demerits outweigh its merits.
Besides the moral point about excluding competent non-POC from
jobs and schools, there is a relational problem. POC who are hired or
admitted due to being POC may become objects of suspicion. Are
they there because of merit or to fill a quota? I often tell my gifted

non-POC graduate students that the odds are against them to find any full-time academic teaching position, especially if they are men. Shelby Steele, who is a black academic, argues that affirmative action encourages self-doubt among black people who are hired or admitted more because of race than because of competence.[57] Thus, affirmative action overall does not add to social harmony, does not empower black people, and does not lead to mutual respect between races.[58]

Another practical problem is the boomerang effect. Affirmative action often springs back to injure the ones it was supposed to help. A prime example of this failure is higher education. For more than three decades, colleges and universities have been admitting students on the basis of racial preferences, which favor black people. That means black students can be admitted to college, universities, and law schools—including some of the most prestigious ones—despite having lower academic rankings than their peers. The motivation for this is good: its proponents believe that, given the history of black people in the United States, they need a leg up or special help in education. Whatever one thinks of this principle, the result has not helped black people overall in higher education. Many writers, such as Dinesh D'Souza,[59] Thomas Sowell,[60] and Heather Mac Donald,[61] have documented the sad trend that these specially admitted black students often later switch to academically easier majors and suffer from disproportionally higher dropout rates overall.

Mismatch: How Affirmative Action Hurts Students It's Intended to Help, and Why Universities Won't Admit It by Richard Sander and Stuart Taylor, makes a sustained case that these racially skewed admission policies have hurt the minorities they were supposed to help while also disadvantaging white people and Asians.[62] Steele is spot on: "racial preferences allow society to leapfrog over the difficult problem of developing blacks to parity with whites and into a cosmetic divert that covers the blemish of disparity."[63]

The American system is sound, if imperfect. Whatever systemic problems now exist are best reformed according to American ideals, not by CRT ideology. The concept of systemic racism, as formulated by CRT, is largely divorced from facts, ignores the dimension of personal values and responsibility, and places the blame unfairly on one racial group, which is, in turn, expected to take responsibility for systemic racism. American citizens of all colors are better served by adhering to the values and perspective of our founding documents and legal reforms, which inspired so many beneficial racial reforms in our nation's history.

MOST
COMBUSTIBLE
TOPICS

CHAPTER FIVE

IDEOLOGY AND TORCHING FREE SPEECH

Ideology injures critical thinking and undermines the moral reflection needed for our American republic to be preserved and to thrive. When judgments are made by preset racial categories, truth is the casualty. Extreme ideological thinking (or better, non-thinking) was captured by George Orwell in *1984* when the protagonist, Winston, is being lectured by O'Brien about reality and the "the Party."

> Only the disciplined mind can see reality, Winston. You believe that reality is something objective, external, existing in its own right. You also believe that the nature of reality is self-evident. When you delude yourself into thinking that you see something, you assume that everyone else sees the same thing as you. But I tell you, Winston, that reality is not external. Reality exists in the human mind, and nowhere else. Not in the individual mind, which

can make mistakes, and in any case soon perishes; only in the mind of the Party, which is collective and immortal. Whatever the Party hold to be the truth is truth. It is impossible to see reality except by looking through the eyes of the Party.[1]

O'Brien further tells Winston, who was a dissenter against the Party, that he must "relearn." It "is an act of self-destruction, and effort of the will. You must humble yourself before you can become sane."[2]

While as yet the state is not shackling people and inflicting on them this state-enforced ideological theory of truth, it is, nevertheless, everywhere to be found—taught in schools, assumed by the news, broadcast on the internet, acted out in films, and is on the lips and in the writings of pundits, politicians, preachers, and other influencers. It must be resisted by dissidents; and you should be a dissident. While Winston was bludgeoned physically and psychologically into loving the Party and Big Brother, we must either resist the blows or use them to strengthen our backbone, transmuting the lies into a deeper resolve to "live not by lies," as Aleksandr Solzhenitsyn, the quintessential dissident under Communism, warned us.[3]

America is not America without the five freedoms guaranteed by the First Amendment to the Constitution ratified in 1791: the freedom of religion, of speech, of press, of assembly, and to petition the government for the redress of wrongs. These are the necessary conditions for rational discourse and political advocacy laid down at the American founding which give America its backbone of liberty and which ensure a marketplace of ideas. We will draw particular attention to freedom of speech, since the forces of CRT ideology threaten to undermine it along with the freedom of religion.

What Is Ideology?

To understand CRT (and politics in general), we must try to understand what *ideology* is and how it works. The term "ideology" can be used as a neutral description with synonyms like "philosophy" or "political outlook."[4] However, ideology can be used in a pejorative sense (by the political left, the right, or the middle) to mean a blinkered and illegitimate outlook driven by vested interests that disqualify it from being rational or true. Conservative critics, such as Russell Kirk[5] and Kenneth Minogue,[6] use the term to refer to leftist or radical views, but Marxists can use it to refer to conservative views.

Consider another way to state the dangers of ideology. One can default to a narrative instead of considering the facts, logic, and history of the situation. The word "narrative" is used constantly today, and it takes several meanings. Like "ideology," it can be used descriptively to mean a story or a way of looking at a state of affairs. The four gospels in the New Testament give a fourfold and consistent narrative of the life of Jesus, for example. Or "narrative" can be used in the sense of ideology, but with an emphasis on the storytelling or history. For example, one narrative says that most problems black people experience today are rooted in slavery, not in other factors since the abolition of slavery. Those factors might include the welfare state's system of trying to alleviate poverty through massive state programs which, at their worst, can reward social problems such as unemployment and illegitimacy.[7] This should be a matter of rational debate, not an *a priori* appeal to narrative. But one can default to narrative reflexively and without reflection as a kind of intellectual twitch. That is ideology in the truth-damaging sense.

Say a white police officer shoots and kills an unarmed black man during an arrest attempt. One narrative invokes systemic racism and immediately judges the police officer guilty and the black man innocent, or at least a victim of injustice. This judgment is usually based on—or is exacerbated by—short video clips lacking context (as most do).[8] The leading factors in this analysis are white vs. black and armed vs. unarmed. But added to this is a narrative of systemic racism, white privilege, white supremacy, and white guilt. In this way, a television viewer may easily and instantly become the judge and jury in a complicated crime scene requiring far more investigation. But one disposed to such judgments can also appeal to statistics interpreted to mean that black people are disproportionately arrested, injured, or shot by police. If so, we find ourselves back in the world of evidence and rationality.

Now consider another narrative concerning the same incident. The officer was justified to shoot the man given high rates of black criminality and because the suspect was resisting arrest, even if he was unarmed. The video clip does not tell the whole story. But one disposed to this judgment can also appeal to statistics concerning the police's treatment of black people compared to other racial groups. And so it goes. We should avoid the ideological mentality that defaults to narrative instead of evaluating situations carefully, especially when combustible issues such as race are involved. We cannot avoid background beliefs that shape our perceptions and expectations, yet those beliefs should be well-grounded in evidence and they should not override the facts on the ground.

Ideology was evident in the response of many American pundits and politicians who, given their leftist views, long denied the killings and mistreatment of the Russian people by the communist government of the USSR (1922–1991). Given their penchant for Marxist utopianism, they ignored the evidence of show trials, state executions, planned famines, and the general brutalization of the people the 1917 Russian Revolution was supposed to liberate.[9] The same was true for existentialist French philosopher Jean-Paul Sartre (1905–1980), who defended the Chinese mass murderer Mao Zedong. He and his partner, Simone de Beauvoir (1908–1986), handed out Maoist pamphlets on the streets of Paris in the midst of the Marxist-Maoist Cultural Revolution (1966–76), which was responsible for the murder of millions of Chinese citizens.[10]

Avoiding ideological narratives requires humility, studiousness, and honesty—three virtues that our media system do not typically encourage.[11] We are too often content with, and even addicted to, soundbites, factoids, talking points, tweets, stock insults, and slogans. Video clips of talking heads battling video clips of other talking heads often substitute for careful analysis and basic research on the topics in question. Ideology should be further explained so that it may be utterly avoided.

The ideologue is certain that she is correct, so she need not reevaluate her basic perspective. It is fixed, certain, and impregnable. She is immune from disproof. She further impugns the motives of those with whom she disagrees. They are "extremists," "racists," "white supremacists," and so on. Or they are "Marxists," "anarchists," "race baiters," and so on. Now, there are real people who fit these categories (Ku Klux Klan members are racists; Karl Marx was a Marxist), but that needs to be demonstrated, not assumed because of ideological tunnel vision. Knowing that someone is a Marxist or neo-Marxist will help predict what she thinks, so one could say, "Yes, that indicates she is a Marxist, and thus she also thinks such-and-such." But one cannot refute an argument by insulting the one arguing. That is to commit the ad hominem logical fallacy.

While ideology can corrupt any political viewpoint, CRT's approach appeals to ideology in the particularly Marxist sense. As Kenneth Minogue puts it "revolutionaries by the end of the [nineteenth] century were using the word 'ideology' to mean any elaborated class point of view, all such viewpoints being partial and distorted except for that of the rising revolutionary class."[12]

Marxism claimed that any political freedoms supposedly won in eighteenth-century Europe—when monarchies gave way to representative governments—were illusory. Workers were still "wage slaves" and "captive to capital." On this view, Marxism claims to have the unique insight into the reality behind the appearances; it sees through the apparent social-economic situation into the reality of ongoing oppression. Thus it possesses a kind of Gnostic illumination about social processes, and thus can reject any criticism as motivated by class interests (capitalist ideology). As the one true view of society, *its ideology* is all-controlling, but it takes the views of its opponents to be ideologically based according to the self-serving illusions perpetuated by the capitalist system. As economist Ludwig von Mises wrote: "Purges are the necessary consequences of the philosophical foundation of Marxian socialism. If you cannot discuss philosophical differences of opinion in the same way you discuss other problems, you must find another solution—through violence and power."[13]

Similarly, the CRT perspective claims that beyond the façade of progress on civil rights and the evidence of achievement by POC lies the "alien power" of racism, which keeps POC in chains that only CRT can truly identify and refute. POC, like earlier Marxists, enjoy a special vantage point.[14] As Horowitz noted in 1999:

> Today the alien power thought by the left to control our destinies is only rarely described as a "ruling class," although it is still perceived as that. Refuted by the history of communist empires, the left has turned to new vocabularies and concepts to rescue it from its defeats. Today the ruling class is identified as the "patriarchy" or the "white male oligarchy," or in disembodied form as the force of "institutional racism" or "white supremacy."[15]

The preferred terms today are "systemic racism," "white supremacy," or "structural racism," but the concept is identical.

Since the ideologue defaults to a preset narrative immune to counterevidence to explain opposition to her views, she need not refute them. In fact, the ideologue scolds and makes demands of her opponents; she cannot hope to convince them, since she takes them to be locked into their views (not realizing she is locked into her views).

Noted sociologist Peter Berger (1929–2017) said that such accounts of knowledge must posit an "epistemological elite" who somehow transcend the conditions that render the ordinary person unable to perceive reality as it truly is. "This elite has the sole custody of truth; everyone else 'just doesn't get it.'"[16] This, of course, is question-begging and can easily lead to authoritarianism for "the knowers" who brook no dissent and who know what other people need. Only those uninitiated can be convinced or, better, indoctrinated. This is why ideologues seek to control education in order to promote and impose only one perspective rather than a free exchange of ideas.[17]

Canceling Free Speech

The CRT ideologue opposes the American ideal of free speech, since CRT claims opponents do not have the right to speak or to be heard. Their ideas are thus deemed thoroughly corrupt and dangerous to the ideologue's ambitions. This can be summarized in what I call "the cancellation fallacy." At the risk of appearing pedantic, I will put it abstractly. Formally, the fallacy is this:

Someone (anyone, but especially a POC) is offended by P (any statement, person, object, process, or event).

Therefore (a), P is wrong.

Therefore (b), the moral wrong committed by one who holds P is serious, such as racism, white supremacism, homophobia, transphobia, or the like.

Therefore (c), whoever affirms P must be cancelled.

Therefore (d), unless others denounce P, they too must be cancelled, since "Silence is violence."

The cancellation fallacy is a synergistic and strenuous effort. It is a high achievement of sophistry. But it suffers from at least five logical fallacies. Let the autopsy begin.

First, it equates taking offense with a proper moral judgment. Thus, it *begs the question* instead of making an argument in its favor. Emotional reactions may be proper or improper, but they cannot ground an argument. Second, it commits the *ad hominem fallacy*. If you offend me, you are a bad person, and bad people cannot give good arguments, which is false. Third, the supposed wrongness is placed into a broad condemning category, such as racism or sexism, and thus commits *the straw man fallacy*. It may offend you that I don't want statues of Abraham Lincoln torn down, but that in itself does not make me a racist. Fourth, the threat of cancellation is a form of intimidation and means punishment if the threat is enacted. This commits the fallacy of *argumentum ad baculum* or "If you don't agree with me, I will hurt you. Therefore, agree with me." Today, this translates as: "Those critical of Critical Race Theory will be cancelled, which means losing your book contract, your employment, your social status, and more." Fifth, to claim that if I do not oppose P, then I must endorse P, commits the fallacy of the argument from silence. Not saying anything ("silence") cannot in itself be used to indict someone. The cancellation fallacy is not good news for reason or for free speech.

CRT ideologues find inspiration in Herbert Marcuse's idea of "repressive tolerance," which he advanced as a leader of the New Left in the 1960s and stated in an influential essay of that name: if the whole social system is a repressive system, then to tolerate it is, in fact, to promote it. Thus, we must *not* tolerate those who grasp the levers of power in society. Rather, we must restrict their speech and freedom in the name of liberation for the oppressed.[18]

Marcuse, given his Marxist assumptions on the systemic nature of oppression, does not advocate the toleration assumed in the freedom of religion, speech, press, assembly, and petition marked out in the First Amendment. For him, such procedures are tainted at the source and cannot produce the kind of social liberation he has in mind (utopia). (Marcuse fled Germany in the 1930s for America, which was the ideal place for *his* free speech.)

The Antifa (or anti-fascist) movement overlaps in ideology with CRT and often serves as the shock troops for violent demonstrations staged by BLM and other pro-CRT groups. They too deny freedom of speech to their "fascist" enemies, since they liken them to Nazis. Antifa writer Mark Bray rejects "the classic liberal phrase incorrectly ascribed to Voltaire that 'I disapprove of what you say, but will defend to the death your right to say it.'" Antifa is "an illiberal politics of social revolution committed to righting the Far Right, not only literal fascists."[19] To that end they dedicate their anti-free speech anarchism.[20]

Lesbian and pagan feminist writer Mary Daly (1928–2010) was ahead of her time when she refused to allow men to speak in her courses at Boston College. More recently, consider footage from the 2019 documentary *No Safe Spaces*.[21] Dr. Bret Weinstein, a liberal white biology professor at Evergreen State College in Washington, was trying to talk with students who had stormed into his classroom because he had refused to observe a request from the administration for white people to stay at home on the annual Day of Absence (a day when students and faculty of the school were to stay home). The idea came from a 1965 play called *Day of Absence* by Douglas Turner Ward, in which all the black people in an imaginary Southern town disappear for one day. The point is that racist societies depend on the people they oppress, and their absence makes this known.

But in 2017, the goal of the Day of Absence at Evergreen was changed to include only white faculty. As Dennis Prager and Mark Joseph put it in their recent book *No Safe Spaces*:

> On the "Day of Absence" Bret Weinstein biked to campus, as was his routine. The first sign that something was amiss came during his first class; an anxious former student flagged him down to tell him that a mob of students outside the building was chanting for him to be fired. When Weinstein tried to engage the protesters, he faced a wall of accusations about racial insensitivity. He tried to reply but found he couldn't finish a sentence. Finally, exasperated, he blurted, "Would you like to hear the answer or not?" Several students shouted, "No!"—and kept on haranguing him.[22]

The students did not want to argue with him; they wanted to silence him—and punish him. They further accosted Weinstein and made it unsafe for him to be present on his own campus for the rest of the term.

Weinstein and his wife, fellow Evergreen State professor Heather Heying, successfully sued the school—receiving a $500,000 settlement—and resigned before the fall term of 2017,[23] although they had been popular teachers and accomplished scholars. Even the liberal *New York Times* editorialized against how Evergreen State College and its students treated Weinstein in a piece called "When the Left Turns on Its Own" by Bari Weiss. She concluded:

Shutting down conservatives has become de rigueur. But now anti-free-speech activists are increasingly turning their ire on free-thinking progressives. Liberals shouldn't cede the responsibility to defend free speech on college campuses to conservatives. After all, without free speech, what's liberalism about?[24]

Indeed, but liberalism (of the old school) is not CRT, which deems liberalism not radical enough to change a systemically racist society. But there is more repression of free speech.

Susan King, dean of the Hussman School of Journalism and Media at the University of North Carolina-Chapel Hill, wrote in an August 1, 2020, memo that there was a "fundamental conflict between efforts to promote racial equity and understandings of structural racism, and efforts to promote diversity of thought. These two things cannot sit side by side without coming into conflict." King wrote the memo because she was expecting Nikole Hannah-Jones to join the UNC faculty. Hannah-Jones is the *New York Times* journalist who engineered the magazine's controversial 1619 Project, which claims that America is based on slavery, and was planning to teach a course based on the project.[25]

CRT claims that society is systemically racist; thus, even the institution of free speech perpetuates that racism, because white people have more control over and access to means of speech and other expression. That was a problem fifty years ago, but is unlikely today, given the number of black journalists, writers, and editors and the influence they wield.[26] At the time of this writing, a black man, Lester Holt, is the anchor for *NBC Nightly News* and has been since 2015. Don Lemon, a gay black man, anchors *Don Lemon Tonight*, a weekly prime-time program on CNN, and serves as a correspondent across CNN/U.S. programming.

Chris Demaske, an associate professor of communication at the University of Washington-Tacoma, writes that CRT scholars have challenged the legitimacy of the First Amendment. They claim that

> instead of helping to achieve healthy and robust debate, the First Amendment actually serves to preserve the inequities of the status quo; there can be no such thing as an objective or content neutral interpretation in law in general or of the First Amendment in particular; some speech should be viewed in terms of the harm it causes, rather than all speech being valued on the basis of it being speech; and there is no "equality" in "freedom" of speech.[27]

Instead of allowing for diverse discourse, CRT thinkers want to penalize some speech because of its toxic nature. Demaske goes on:

> In general, these scholars argue that there is no societal value in protecting speech that targets already oppressed groups. They also question the logic of using the First Amendment to protect speech that not only has no social value, but also is socially and psychologically damaging to minority groups.[28]

And who, one wonders, determines what has "no social value"? In an essay about controversies about racism in campus newspapers, Ibram X. Kendi wrote, "Just like we should not have the freedom to enslave people, we should not have the freedom to publish untruths about people."[29] This is a false analogy, since slavery should not be permitted at all, but the publication of untruths about people cannot be avoided in a free society—and remedies for it already exist in libel law. Kendi's trope sounds noble, but the First Amendment ensures freedom of speech, not freedom from falsehood, and not freedom from ideas that he does not agree with.

Kendi is quick to label views he disagrees with as racist. To him, anything that fails to fit his extreme model of being "antiracist" is racist. Racist writings exist, and are odious; but censoring speech of which one does not approve is odious as well. Libel and slander laws cover the more egregious falsehoods, letters to the editor and op-ed pieces expand the discourse, good editors will not allow rank error, and we have a variety of sources to draw from in forming our views. An unfettered marketplace of ideas allows for multiple viewpoints to be articulated. Still, the messiness and raucousness of free speech—which allows for the publication of "untruths about people," as Kendi fears—is far better than preemptive ideological control over intellectual discourse, especially when it comes to something as contentious as race.

CRT thinkers and their fellow travelers invented the term "hate speech," supposedly to protect oppressed groups from verbal abuse. However, they have used it to silence or muffle dissenting views. Or, as they would put it, "to empower oppressed groups." Speech codes limit what students can say on state university campuses or restrict them to expressing ideas in certain areas. Although federal courts have issued rulings saying some speech codes violate the First Amendment, they are common on university campuses where they are defended as necessary to protect racial and sexual minorities.

The First Amendment is not absolute in the sense of allowing any speech whatsoever. The Supreme Court in *Chaplinsky v. New Hampshire* (1942) determined that the right to free speech does not extend to discourse characterized as "the lewd and obscene, the profane, the libelous, and the insulting or 'fighting words.'"[30] Nevertheless, as Justice Antonin Scalia (1936–2016) explained for the Court in *R.A.V. v. St. Paul* (1992), the First Amendment "prevents the government from proscribing speech because of its disapproval of the ideas" contained in that speech.[31] This is the "viewpoint neutrality" principle that the Court has strongly defended. It was articulated by Justice Oliver Wendell Holmes in a 1929 dissent to another ruling: "Speech that demeans on the basis of race, ethnicity, gender, religion, age, disability, or any other similar ground is hateful; but the proudest boast of our free speech jurisprudence is that we protect the freedom to express 'the thought that we hate.'"[32]

Hateful speech exists, but who determines what is hateful and what is not hateful, and who would enforce banning "hate speech"? I favor the view Holmes expressed in his dissent in *Abrams v. United States* (1919): "The best test of truth is the power of the thought to get itself accepted in the competition of the market."[33] This may not be "the best test for *truth*," but it is a necessary condition for the free exchange of ideas that is the most likely to result in the discovery of truth for those who care to investigate wisely. Banning certain viewpoints disallows profitable debate. Supreme Court Justice Louis Brandeis famously said, "Publicity is justly commended as a remedy for social and industrial diseases. Sunlight is said to be the best of disinfectants; electric light the most efficient policeman."[34]

As John Stuart Mill wrote in his classic work, *On Liberty*:

> He who knows only his own side of the case, knows little of that. His reasons may be good, and no one may have been able to refute them. But if he is equally unable to refute the reasons on the opposite side; if he does not so much as know what they are, he has no ground for preferring either opinion.[35]

Mill opposed the silencing of opinions in principle,

But the peculiar evil of silencing the expression of an opinion is, that it is robbing the human race, posterity as well as the existing generation; those who dissent from the opinion, still more than those who hold it. If the opinion is right, they are deprived of the opportunity of exchanging error for truth: if wrong, they lose, what is almost as great a benefit, the clearer perception and livelier impression of truth, produced by its collision with error.[36]

Going even further back into the history of philosophy, we find noble Socrates, who elevates the value of dialogue which has truth as the goal.

If, therefore, you are a person of the same sort as myself, should be glad to continue questioning you: if not, I can let it drop. Of what sort am I? One of those who would be glad to be refuted if I say anything untrue, and glad to refute anyone else who might speak untruly; but just as glad, mind you, to be refuted as to refute, since I regard the former as the greater benefit, in proportion as it is a greater benefit for oneself to be delivered from the greatest evil than to deliver someone else. For I consider that a man cannot suffer any evil so great as a false opinion on the subjects of our actual argument.[37]

The CRT ideology pits itself against the entire modern Western tradition of free speech and rational dialogue. That long and arduous story dates from the oppressive religious authorities who decreed that "error had no rights" to the glories of the First Amendment.

But the ideologue—CRT advocate or otherwise—cannot tolerate an open marketplace of ideas, since he or she rejects the concept of any rational dialogue that might lead to true beliefs that correspond to objective reality. He rejects "neutrality." To an ideologue, the jury is always rigged against oppressed groups; thus, the oppressors should not be given the opportunity to speak, since that would only further their oppressive power. In CRT, much is made of "implicit bias," which is used to supposedly find unconscious racist motives in whites.[38] While this does happen, the idea is frequently used to disqualify any criticisms of CRT or any evidence that a particular white person is not a racist. If so, the case is rigged.

In rejecting neutrality and open argument based on reason and evidence, CRT advocates betray their belief that they cannot win arguments. They can only vilify and silence opponents. As Marx and Engels wrote in *The Communist Manifesto*:

> You must, therefore, confess that by "individual" you mean no other person than the bourgeois, than the middle-class owner of property. This person must, indeed, be swept out of the way, and made impossible.[39]

Neutrality and Objectivity

But what about "neutrality" in law and public discourse? CRT thinkers, on the one hand, claim there is no neutrality in matters of race in America. The deck is stacked against black people and POC in general. So they assert their theoretical views as a substitute. On the other hand, to justify their views, CRT thinkers need to cite evidence and marshal arguments, an endeavor that assumes some cognitive ability to assess reality apart from ideology.[40] For example, in the book *Introducing Critical Race Theory*, in the section titled "How Much Racism Is There in the World?" the authors cite several disparities in education, income, incarceration, and so on, between white people and African Americans.[41] But to make their argument, these citations must be factual—that is, they must agree with objective reality. There is some objective or neutral standard to which they must appeal. We cannot create our own facts nor mint our own validity in reasoning. Further, the authors assume, but do not demonstrate, that these adverse disparities are the result of racism. Notwithstanding, disparities in achievement have multiple causes, as I argued earlier. To make this case, the authors would need to appeal to the proper selection and interpretation of data. Again, they need to aspire to neutrality or objectivity. The term "objectivity" can be used in two ways, and addressing this might clear up confusion.

No one is objective in the sense that he or she has no passions, interests, prejudices, or biases. However, if we aspire to gain knowledge (justified and true beliefs), then we ought to aim to be disinterested in the classic use of that term, which does not mean "uninterested." To be disinterested requires that we try to keep in check any inclination that might distort or ignore the truth for self-serving purposes. The adage "Follow the truth wherever it leads" expresses this perfectly. As philosopher J. P. Moreland notes:

> But if truth really matters after all, then it follows that rationality also is crucial to a life well lived. Why? Because if we want a life built on truth, we want to be sure that our worldview consists of the highest percentage of true beliefs and the lowest percentage of false ones.[42]

So, while we cannot be totally objective, we can aspire to discover objective truths through disinterested reasoning. This need not exclude passion for causes. But the ideologue cannot truly appeal to the objective truth, since he claims that "neutrality" and "objectivity" are fictions propped up by the "ruling class" (pure Marxism) or by "white supremacy/white privilege" (neo-Marxist, CRT). Someone interviewed on the NPR program *All Things Considered* asserted that "objective truth" was a "white supremacist" idea. She, however, asserted that as an objective truth and so refuted herself.

No one should support the *ideas* offered by genuinely hateful groups. They are unkind and untrue. However, the American spirit allows free speech even when it is offensive speech. The alternative is *censorship according to ideology*. Banning "hate speech" would, indeed, muzzle some obnoxious, incendiary, and intellectually worthless or even dangerous speech. But the byproduct would be banning speech that is not obnoxious and worthless but, rather, only offensive to the ones who control the discourse.

Recently, numerous speakers—conservative and liberal, but mostly conservative—have been deplatformed, either through being banned by social media or not allowed to speak at colleges and universities. I will address the latter problem. A speaker is invited to campus, but not allowed to speak because he is shouted down or physically assaulted. These speakers are not neo-Nazis or Ku Klux Klan members but people such as the social scientist Charles Murray and author Heather Mac Donald. Before conservative author Ben Shapiro spoke at the University of California-Berkeley in 2017, "concrete barriers had been erected, nearby campus buildings had been shut down, and a secure perimeter had been established."[43] The event did not trigger an incident, but it shows there is no safe and open "marketplace of ideas" at UC-Berkeley.

The ideologue's opponents must be neutralized by one means or another. In this, she appeals (whether overtly or covertly) to what Marxists call "false consciousness." To have false consciousness is more than being errant or mistaken; it is, rather, a whole way of thinking and being in the world that is wrong, root and branch. Those not awakened to the meaning of history as class struggle—whether oppressed or oppressors—experience false consciousness resulting from the economic conditions of being a worker or an owner. This idea is further employed to dismiss and derogate the perspectives of those not "woke" to the injustices of race and gender in America. Those who are not Marxists or neo-Marxists will not invoke "false consciousness," but, at their worst, simply dismiss and derogate their political opponents as well.

An ideological approach to social issues and politics stultifies critical thinking, retards disinterested analysis, and fails to take alternative views seriously, since it deems them the product of malign or obtuse factors. Some ideologues (especially of the CRT type) deem opposing views as toxic and thus worthy of preemptive censure. Ideologues of all sorts will abound until the End, but a nation that values, upholds, and defends the freedom of speech enshrined in our First Amendment has the best opportunity for the truth to emerge through spirited dialogue and debate. The marketplace of ideas must be kept open to all interlocuters. May the best arguments win!

CHAPTER SIX

SHOULD WE SET FLAMES TO THE FREE MARKET?

Racism, Economics, and Reparations

Critical Race Theory is anti-capitalist, since it deems capitalism to be a system that unfairly benefits white people at the expense of black people and other POC. During her reflections on the riots of 2020, longtime communist activist, celebrity, and professor Angela Davis said, "There is no capitalism without racism."[1] She might also have said, "There is no communism without racism," since racism is a sin that afflicts people in all economic systems. Natalie Jeffers, the cofounder of BLM in the United Kingdom, "urged her followers to: 'Fight racism with solidarity. Fight capitalism with socialism. We must organize—dedicate ourselves to revolutionary politic power.'"[2] CRT claims that capitalism is a powerful engine for racism and that it is fueled by racism. Much of the sound and fury on display after George Floyd's death in the summer of 2020 was aimed at capitalism. Some deemed the vandalism and theft against businesses as blows against the capitalist system itself.

Before that, Ibram X. Kendi put it clearly in an interview with *TIME*: "You can't separate capitalism from racism, that they were birthed during the same period in the same area and have grown together, damaged together, and will one day die together."[3] Here it sounds like Kendi believes that when capitalism dies, then racism will die. But in his book, *How To Be an Antiracist,* Kendi claims that capitalism is a *sufficient condition* for racism: if capitalism, then racism. However, capitalism is not a *necessary condition* for racism, since he grants that noncapitalist systems, such as Cuba's, can be racist as well. Thus, the right kind of non-capitalist system *allows for* racism but does not *require* it in the way he believes capitalism does. Nevertheless, Kendi seems optimistic about economic change indeed—with the death of capitalism will come the death of racism, but only if the noncapitalist order is combined with his prescribed practice of antiracism.[4]

Racism exists in socialist countries as well. The writings of Marx, Engels, and Lenin are littered with racist statements; in addition to their other ills, socialist countries struggle with racism too.[5] I will argue below that there is nothing about capitalism that encourages racism, but that the problem lies in the human heart, as Jesus said (Mark 7:21–23).

We have noted that three of the founders of BLM identify as Marxists and, as such, are anticapitalist. In a statement that was later scrubbed from its website, BLM stated flatly that it aims to "disrupt" the traditional family, which is a key plank in *The Communist Manifesto.*

We disrupt the Western-prescribed nuclear family structure requirement by supporting each other as extended families and "villages" that collectively care for one another, especially our children, to the degree that mothers, parents, and children are comfortable.[6]

Communists believe the family is a bad effect of capitalism and should be abolished in favor of the collective raising of children in a socialist state. BLM agrees. However, Christians and Jews know that the heterosexual and monogamous family is a divinely authorized institution meant for human flourishing (Genesis 1–2; Matthew 19:1–6).[7]

CRT is a culturally Marxist ideology that wants to leave nothing as it was before, including a free-market system. Marx, of course, wanted to abolish capitalism through the proletariat revolution. But why attack the free market as racist? We will answer that question and then defend the free market against the socialist alternative. First, we need rough definitions, realizing most economic situations are mixtures of socialism and free enterprise, with one having more influence than the other.

A free-market economy is one in which economic activity is based on individuals buying and selling goods and services in an open field of possibilities (the market), whose operations are bounded by law. This means low taxes, which allow for maximum economic activity and the goods that come from it. The state is minimal, since it is not in the business of regulating the economy by force. This is often called "capitalism," a term coined by Marx to refer to an intrinsically exploitative system. I will refer to this as "the free-enterprise system" or "the free-market economy," as those terms are more accurate.

Socialism, on the other hand, requires the exchange of goods and services through the central planning of the civil government, using confiscation, regulation, and redistribution. It takes over important spheres of life, such as healthcare, education, transportation, agriculture, and so on. High taxes are required, since the state needs the money that it cannot earn itself. Socialism requires a maximal state (or statism) for all these operations.

Capitalism and Racism: A Match Made in Hell?

To CRT thinkers, capitalism supports racism. The core idea is twofold. First, capitalism grew in America during the trans-Atlantic slave trade and thus gave white Americans far more wealth than black Americans. Second, white people today in a capitalist system still have more wealth (on average) than black people, which is unjust. Therefore, capitalism supports racism, which disadvantages black Americans. Further, capitalism should be abolished for the sake of racial equity. The alternative is socialism.

The free-market system could not have *created* slavery, since slavery has existed since the Fall and under different economies and governments. Thomas Sowell gives perspective.

> If longevity and universality are criteria, then slavery must be among the leading candidates for the most appalling of all human institutions, for it existed around the world, for thousands of years, as far back as the history of the human species goes. Yet its full scope is often grossly underestimated today, when slavery is so often discussed as if it were confined to one race enslaving another race, when in fact slavery existed virtually wherever it was feasible for some human beings to enslave other human beings—including in many, if not most, cases people of their own race. This was as true in Europe and Asia as it was in Africa, or in the Western Hemisphere before Columbus' ships ever appeared on the horizon.[8]

Today, the Chinese Communist Party enslaves about two million Uyghur Muslims, using "totalitarian tactics like pervasive surveillance, thought control, ideological reeducation, forced birth control, and compulsory labor."[9] Moreover, throughout history, slavery has not been based essentially on racial animosity, but on the willingness and ability of some in Group A to enslave some in Group B.[10] For example, as Sowell observes, "An estimated one-third of the 'free persons of color' in New Orleans were slaveowners and thousands of these slaveowners volunteered to fight for the Confederacy in the Civil War."[11]

While slavery and the free market *coexisted* under slavery, that hardly entails that a free market leads to slavery, endorses slavery, or cannot exist without slavery. Moreover, slavery does not support the flourishing of a free market, as Joseph Bast, founder of the free-market think tank the Heartland Institute, notes: "Slavery is obviously at odds with the principles and demands of capitalism [such as:] self-ownership, freedom to trade, voluntary contracts, and equality."[12]

Additionally, it was primarily the Southern slave-owning states that benefited from slavery under capitalism. The Northern states forbade slavery, and their economies did not flourish from it. Thus, to say that American white people as a whole benefitted from slavery is untrue. Some did and some did not. As Sowell has shown, slavery in the South was no boon to the economy when compared with the North, because slavery has both advantages and substantial disadvantages economically. To think that the American economy as a whole was built on slavery, as the 1619 Project claims, is flatly untrue. The slaves' labor was stolen from them, but slavery exacted costs on the owners as well and was not—simply on economic grounds—a good investment over the long term.[13] Moreover, "it is apparent empirically that the incomes of the white population of the United States have been lowest in the region in which slavery existed."[14] This fact undermines "the belief that non-slave-owning white people benefitted economically from slavery."[15]

After slavery, from about 1870–90, African Americans were enjoying their new freedoms and were beginning to advance in a free-market society. The free-enterprise system was not an engine of racism, even if white people who had prospered because of slavery were able to keep their ill-gotten gains under this system. As Bast notes:

> Jim Crow laws did not arise from institutions of capitalism or precapitalist feudal society but were invented and used by opponents of integration to exclude African-Americans from mainstream political and economic life.[16]

These laws were statist *restrictions on the free market*, since they disallowed white people and black people from associating at some businesses. The profit motive encouraged some large businesses to hire black people. As William Julius Wilson noted in *The Declining Significance of Race*,

> Indeed, the determination of industrialists to ignore racial norms of exclusion and to hire black workers was one of the main reasons why the industry-wide unions reversed their racial policies and actively recruited black workers during the New Deal era. Prior to this period the overwhelming majority of unskilled and semiskilled blacks were nonunionized and were available as lower-paid labor or as strikebreakers.[17]

Free enterprise helped desegregate and integrate the workforce, as opposed to perpetuating racism. However, racism can be perpetuated through discriminatory laws that have nothing to do with free enterprise, as with Jim Crow. And, of course, racists can be racists in a free market—as they can in a socialist country. The unjust "redlining" that went on after World War II which segregated communities and limited black people's access to loans and housing had nothing to do with the free market per se and everything to do with bad governmental policies.[18]

A racist may get rich, but his wealth need not be based on the economic exploitation of any POC. Even if he dislikes black people or Hispanics, he may hire them if it pays. White employers under apartheid in South Africa (1948–94) often hired black people at higher rates and in higher positions than the government legally allowed. This was not because of their love of black people, but because it served their profit interests. As Sowell observes:

> While racists, by definition, prefer their own race to other races, individual racists—like other people—tend to prefer themselves most of all. That is what led to widespread violations of apartheid laws by white employers and landlords in competitive industries in South Africa. It cost nothing for white South Africans to vote for candidates promoting white supremacy. But the costs of refusing to hire black workers who would make their business profitable could be considerable. Moreover, the cost of refusing to hire them when their competitors in the product market were hiring them, and therefore could have lower costs of doing business—enabling competitors to undercut the product prices of employers who failed to hire black workers—exposed those who obeyed apartheid laws to the risk of losing profits and potentially losing their whole business.[19]

The profit motive may override the effects of an individual's racism to some extent.[20] As Scottish economist Adam Smith noted in 1776, in market situations, self-interest (even selfishness) can serve a common good.

> It is not from the benevolence of the butcher, the brewer, or the baker that we expect our dinner, but from their regard to their own interest. We address ourselves, not to their humanity, but to their self-love, and never talk to them of our own necessities, but of their advantages. Nobody but a beggar chooses to depend chiefly upon the benevolence of his fellow-citizens.[21]

Smith was a moral philosopher in addition to being an economist; the distinction was not hard and fast in his day. In *Theory of Moral Sentiments* (1759), he argued that sympathy is the key social virtue and should be brought into all neighborly relations, economic or otherwise. However, he realized that the market can provide benefits even when people are motivated more by self-love than by sympathy.

Socialism and the Information Problem

A fundamental problem with socialism—besides its confiscation of individual wealth and its imperious control of private property—is its information problem in administering the socialist system. Socialism stultifies efficient economic information needed for the distribution of goods and services. Instead of letting the market decide prices and the availability of goods and services, socialism requires a *command economy*. Prices are set by the civil government and centralized bureaucratic authority. Why not "spread the wealth around," as Barack Obama told Joe the Plumber in 2011? "The answer is that we must 'spread the knowledge around.'"[22] Central planning through a command economy is incapable of that.

A free market allows and facilitates an unlimited number of buyers and sellers to respond to each other, given the law of supply and demand. Prices serve as units of information to be exchanged. If prices go up, we know that demand exceeds supply and vice versa. Wages send signals through the market as well and are subject to variation given changing economic conditions. This information exchange is muted by socialism, since the distribution of goods and services and the rate of salaries are controlled by the state, which is a centralized authority incapable of knowing the relevant economic conditions on the ground. It is a blind guide, and it generates shortages even when there is no scarcity of goods. In the USSR, warehouses were filled with goods that never made it where they were needed simply because there was no market to give the appropriate signals through prices.[23] As Sowell notes:

> In centrally planned economies, we have seen the planners overwhelmed by the task of trying to set literally millions of prices—and keep changing those prices in response to innumerable and often unforeseeable changes in circumstances. It was not remarkable that they failed so often. What was remarkable was that anyone had expected them to succeed, given the vast amount of knowledge that would have had to be marshaled and mastered in one place by one set of people at one time, in order to make such an arrangement work.[24]

History, facts, and logic shout at us that socialist central planning will not help any economy. The information problem is a constitutive flaw of socialism.[25] It is an unworkable system. The pied piper has no clothes and always plays out of tune and off the beat—an unsightly, cacophonous, and ungainly combination.

Since good citizens seek the most benefit for society economically, while protecting fair exchange through law, they should not support a socialist economy that is blind to the most important economic indicators that make possible free and prosperous financial exchange (Jeremiah 29:7; Matthew 5:16–18). No great cosmic vision of equality and sharing can overcome these facts.[26]

The free market will spawn no utopia (given our *constrained vision* of humanity), but socialist planning and control have brought and will bring many dystopias (and worse). The socialist president Hugo Chávez turned a prosperous Venezuela into an economic nightmare. As U.S. Sen. Rand Paul notes with respect to its oil:

> Venezuela was so rich with oil that it took some time for socialism to completely destroy its once-vibrant economy. Even to this day Venezuela still has the largest oil reserves in the world, even greater than Saudi Arabia's. They just can't get it out of the ground because socialism has destroyed the pricing system, and endless government spending and debt caused hyperinflation that has destroyed its currency.[27]

While socialism typically impoverishes countries, a free market typically lifts countries and people out of poverty, sometimes dramatically so. For example, Taiwan, Singapore, and Hong Kong have all abandoned socialism and moved toward free market practices, and have grown more prosperous as a result. Millions have been taken out of poverty in India and even China with the implementation of more economic freedoms.[28]

Socialism against Freedom

Worse yet, the vaunted ideals of empowering the working class or the unemployed and establishing an economic democracy cannot be met under socialism. As the ex-liberal professor Michael Rectenwald observes, not only does socialism fail to allocate resources efficiently (or at all), it also fails at "the economic representation of the people it claims to champion." Without pricing mechanisms, economic actors lack a voice to advance their desires in the market. "Production and distribution must be based on the non-democratic decision-making of centralized authorities."[29]

Nobel Prize-winning economist Milton Friedman (1912–2006) argued that socialism is incompatible with a free citizenry, since the state must either seize or regulate nearly all aspects of life, leaving little room for personal freedoms. This renders the idea of "democratic socialism" (championed by U.S. Sen. Bernie Sanders and U.S. Rep. Alexandria Ocasio-Cortez) an oxymoron, since the state ends up dominating the economy and either eliminating or restricting private property. On the other hand, free enterprise allows for political freedoms, although it does not insure them. In other words, the free market is a *necessary* condition for political freedom, but not a *sufficient* condition. Authoritarian governments have sometimes allowed free enterprise but have stifled other important measures of freedom relating to speech and religion.[30] From 1921–28, Lenin allowed for some free-market development in the USSR—called the New Economic Policy—because his state-planned, command economy measures were starving the country.[31] China has allowed more economic freedoms, which have helped many, but it remains totalitarian, given its Marxist anchorage.

Socialism Lite for POC?

While many Americans are still wary of full-blown socialism (but ever less so),[32] they may support socialist measures to help those mired in poverty, many of whom are black or other POC. Consider two such measures: minimum wage laws and increased taxes on "the rich." When the state requires a minimum wage (which is not set by the free market), it necessarily shrinks the number of jobs available. An employer who would hire someone at nine dollars an hour may not hire *anyone* at fifteen dollars an hour. This increases unemployment among low-skilled individuals. Sowell explains the real minimum wage:

> Making it illegal to pay less than a given amount does not make a worker's productivity worth that amount—and, if it is not, that worker is unlikely to be employed. Yet minimum wage laws are almost always discussed politically in terms of the benefits they confer on workers receiving those wages. Unfortunately, the real minimum wage is always zero, regardless of the laws, and that is the wage that many workers receive in the wake of the creation or escalation of a government-mandated minimum wage, because they either lose their jobs or fail to find jobs when they enter the labor force.[33]

Further, the idea that low-wage workers typically support a family and need a government-set wage to do so is bogus. As Sowell notes:

"Only 15 percent of minimum-wage workers are supporting themselves and a dependent, the kind of person envisioned by those who advocate a 'living wage.'"[34] Those working for low wages are often younger and earn more as they develop skills later in life. Sowell summarizes: "When all is said and done, most empirical studies indicate that minimum wage laws reduce employment in general, and especially the employment of younger, less skilled, and minority workers."[35] That is hardly good news for the poor, whether POC or not.[36] The free market gives more opportunities for employment and more freedom to employers.

Socialists and their fellow travelers inveigh against capitalism because of inequalities in wealth. One way to correct this supposed injustice is by levying high taxes on "the rich," who "should pay their fair share"—as we hear every election cycle.

Tax policy is complicated, but one anti-free market myth can be refuted. Higher tax *rates* on high income earners do not, as a rule, generate more tax *revenue*. Tax cuts on the wealthy often lead to more tax revenue because (1) the wealthy invest more instead of hiding money in tax shelters when tax rates are high, and (2) the wealthy make more money, so they pay more total taxes and also provide more goods and services, since their businesses tend to do better, which benefits everyone. Tax *revenues* went up when President Ronald Reagan cut tax *rates* for the highest incomes (1980–88). Sowell notes that "before the series of tax cuts that began in the Reagan administration, 37 percent of all income tax revenues came from the top 5 percent of income earners. After a series of 'tax cuts for the rich' over the years had reduced the highest marginal tax rate to 35 percent by 2004, now more than half of all income tax revenues came from the top 5 percent."[37] This is a repeated pattern: *decrease* tax rates on the wealthy and this will *increase* tax revenues overall.

The concept of "the rich paying their fair share" is based on two false assumptions. First is the zero-sum assumption. Wealth is a static quantity. If some have a larger share of the economic pie, that is because the rest have a smaller share. It has been taken from them.

But economic wealth in a free market is not a static quantity; it is rather a dynamic force. Wealth can be *created* through innovation, and those who benefit financially are not defrauding anyone as long as they have not broken any laws to get where they are. Good software adds value and wealth to the economy. I take it that multibillionaire Bill Gates has not stolen anything from anyone to make his billions. He has provided goods, services, and jobs for hundreds of millions of people. He has more than he needs, but that does not mean that he has taken any of it from someone who is needy.[38] He has also engaged in massive philanthropy, an activity reserved for the exceptionally rich.

The second false assumption lurking behind the desire to "soak the rich" is that income inequalities—especially large inequalities—are *inherently unfair*. Thus, they need to be *leveled* by taxation and the redistribution of wealth by the state. This is untrue. If a drug lord in Mexico is rich and his addicted consumers are not, then this inequity is unjust, but only because it is criminal. The wealth of Bill Gates (white) or Jay-Z (black) vastly exceeds that of most people, but the sheer discrepancy in wealth lacks moral significance.

But is not vast wealth a scandal, given the sheer existence of poverty and other inequalities? There is no clear reasoning why. Harry Frankfurt summarizes this point:

> The fundamental error of economic egalitarianism lies in supposing that it is morally important whether one person has less than another, regardless of how much either of

them has and regardless also of how much utility each derives from what he has.[39]

It is not necessarily true that someone with a smaller income has more significant unmet needs than someone who is wealthier.[40] That depends on multiple factors, and fixating on incomes alone is a limiting and erroneous measure.

Many claim that the free-enterprise system is "based on greed" or tends to make people greedy. But Jesus said that greed comes *out of the heart* and is what makes someone unclean (Mark 7:22–23). The free market does not generate greed more effectively than socialism, since it comes from inside a person. You can be greedy with little or greedy with much. Socialism *requires* envy, however, given its rejection of large (or any) income inequality.[41] A free-market economy *allows for* greed, but does not require it. And, as noted by Adam Smith, even greed may benefit others in a free market.

The Socialist Alternative, Race, and Reparations

Even if we grant that the free-enterprise system has done a disservice to black people, it does not follow that socialism would be any better for them—or for anyone else. Remember that a realistic view of politics is that of the constrained vision, which aligns with the Judeo-Christian account of our humanity, culture, and the state. Finding injustices in one system does not imply that these injustices will be eliminated or lessened by another system. Other injustices may replace and exceed the previous injustices. This is true for socialism.

And the track record of socialism—on every indicator—is nothing to brag about. The USSR regime was far worse than Czarist Russia. Mao Zedong exceeded the evils of his predecessors by many orders of magnitude. And so it goes. But might reparations help black people in America, even if we do not embrace outright socialism?

Do black people in the United States deserve reparations because their ancestors were enslaved and thus deprived of wages and wealth, and because they were further economically discriminated against in the Jim Crow era and beyond? Those who claim that America is systemically racist advance reparations as a measure to make it more equitable.

This question of reparations has several dimensions. They divide into questions of moral principle and questions of pragmatic possibility. But first, to definitions.

The word *reparation* is roughly equivalent to *restitution* or *recompense*. A reparation is a good given by one offending party to another disadvantaged party to compensate for or address a previous wrongdoing. Some cases are clear-cut, as in biblical law: "Whoever steals an ox or a sheep and slaughters it or sells it must pay back five head of cattle for the ox and four sheep for the sheep" (Exodus 21:1). The restitution goes beyond replacing the stolen good to penalizing the thief, who must pay back more than he stole.[42] Jesus commended the repentance and restitution offered by the corrupt tax collector, Zacchaeus, who after having fellowship with Jesus, cried out, "Look, Lord! Here and now I give half of my possessions to the poor, and if I have cheated anybody out of anything, I will pay back four times the amount" (Luke 19:8).

In these cases, the wrongdoer directly gives restitution or reparation to the one wronged. Thus, justice is served. But what of reparation regarding *groups*? Consider the internment of about 120,000 Japanese Americans on our own soil during World War II. The federal government, fearing that Japanese Americans might be more loyal to Japan than America, took these citizens from their homes, confiscated their property, and put them in detention camps until the end of the war. Long afterward, the United States government admitted the wrongness of these actions and offered reparations to those living who had been interned. About 80,000 survivors were paid $20,000 each in reparations.[43]

The point is not to consider whether the amount paid was adequate (it was not), but whether the principle involved was just. It seems it was. Those interned were easily identifiable as Japanese and the perpetrator was clearly identifiable as the United States government.[44] The German government still pays reparations to Jews who were imprisoned and oppressed by the Nazis. Those who oppressed the Jews (the Nazis) are not paying the reparations, but those who directly experienced the oppression are receiving them.[45] These two cases of reparations for Japanese Americans and Jews trade on the right principles. Now on to reparations to black people in the United States.

All those directly afflicted by the evils of slavery are long dead and cannot be compensated in this world. All those who sinfully enslaved them are long dead and cannot be punished in this world. Some of those benefitting economically (white people) and suffering economically (black people) during Jim Crow are still alive. But this does not include all black people or all white people in America today, and sorting it out is impossible. Ta-Nehisi Coates and others argue that since black people were sometimes not allowed to fairly receive federal loans for housing, this further adds weight to the need for reparations.[46] (This is called redlining: "a discriminatory practice that puts services [financial and otherwise] out of reach for residents of certain areas based on race or ethnicity."[47])

But how could these people or their descendants be identified and compensated today? Not all black people today were affected by this. The fact that the civil government created a problem does not mean that the civil government can fix it, as noted earlier.[48]

Still, some argue that even if black people were not directly hurt by slavery or Jim Crow, the *ongoing effects* of racism merit reparations. Even if white people did not directly hurt black people, they owe black people something, nevertheless, given their unearned "white privilege."[49] This idea requires the concept of collective and racial guilt. White people are guilty because of their race and because of their ancestry. Black people are entitled to reparations because of their race and because of their ancestry. Or we might insist that the American government as a whole is guilty, so it should pay reparations—not white people in particular.

Some will appeal to biblical texts to support the idea of collective guilt. For example, Daniel confesses the sins of his people, not merely his own sins.

> Lord, the great and awesome God, who keeps his covenant of love with those who love him and keep his commandments, we have sinned and done wrong. We have been wicked and have rebelled; we have turned away from your commands and laws. We have not listened to your servants the prophets, who spoke in your name to our kings, our princes and our ancestors, and to all the people of the land (Daniel 9:4–6).

But making Daniel an apologetic for reparations fails. He does judge sin as collective, so that the whole nation needs to repent. However, he is speaking of sins committed in the present tense, not of a sinful institution or institutions that had long ended. Daniel asks for mercy. "We do not make requests of you because we are righteous, but because of your great mercy" (9:18). He appeals to God's grace and does not call for compensation for sins. That was not his situation.

While collective guilt was real to Daniel, the Bible stresses individual responsibility. The prophet Ezekiel prophesied:

> GOD's Message to me: "What do you people mean by going around the country repeating the saying,
>> 'The parents ate green apples,
>> The children got the stomachache?'
> "As sure as I'm the living God, you're not going to repeat this saying in Israel any longer. Every soul—man, woman, child—belongs to me, parent and child alike. You die for your own sin, not another's." (Ezekiel 18:1–4 MSG)[50]

But even if collective guilt is real (or was real during biblical times), that in itself does not justify reparations. Guilt should be admitted where necessary and repentance should be enacted where necessary. But reparations demand far more than admitting guilt and being repentant. They involve questionable principles of justice and massive economic outlays.

What *pragmatic good* might reparations do? For the sake of argument, let us grant that reparations are due to American black people; how might they be given and what effect might they have?

First is the problem of identifying which black people should receive the reparations. Many black people in the United States have no American ancestry of slavery. Thus, to compensate them seems unfair. For example, on November 2, 2021, Winsome Sears, a naturalized citizen from Jamaica, was elected lieutenant governor of Virginia.[51] She has no ancestry of American slavery. Should she receive reparations? How would black people verify their slave heritage? The prospects are slim, but some might be able to do it.

Second, given the generally deleterious effects of the Great Society on African Americans—during which huge amounts of money were given (directly or indirectly) to black people—why should we surmise that more wealth transfers through redistribution would benefit black people overall now? The blight of black underachievement goes far deeper than a lack of funds or racism; it reaches to agency, values, culture, and character, as Thomas Sowell, Jason Riley, Shelby Steele, and others have argued. An infusion of money would directly help some black people (and would help many chronically low-income white people, as in Appalachia), but there is no guarantee that reparations in general would solve—let alone ameliorate—the kinds of problems the black community experiences.

Third, would reparations be given to all black people, irrespective of their net wealth and income? Would black business tycoons, such as billionaire Oprah Winfrey, receive reparations when they obviously have benefitted tremendously from the American economic system and are in no need of more money?[52] Would Ta-Nehisi Coates—a well-off and bestselling author who wrote a book to teach his son that America is against him because he is black—receive them?[53] He has argued for reparations before Congress and in an influential essay in the *Atlantic*.[54] However, according to identity politics, since all black people are members of an oppressed *group*, they are all entitled to reparations. Such is the intellectual poverty of identity politics.

Fourth, as I write, America's economy is in crisis, given high inflation (which hurts the poor disproportionately, since they don't have the discretionary income of those more wealthy), supply chain problems, shortages of various products, and worker shortages. The federal government is printing fiat currency as fast as the presses can run, which contributes to inflation.[55] As of October 20, 2021, the ever-increasing national debt stood[56] at $28.8 trillion.[57] The massive outlay of funds needed for reparations would exacerbate this debt and would, on balance, not benefit the American people as a whole or the black community in particular, since increased debt diminishes the strength of the currency in trade, stifles economic growth, and increases unemployment. Consider the Bible: "The rich rule over the poor, and the borrower is slave to the lender" (Proverbs 22:7). The Apostle Paul advises: "Let no debt remain outstanding, except the continuing debt to love one another, for whoever loves others has fulfilled the law" (Romans 13:8).

If the free market were torched for the sake of ending or lessening racism and replaced by socialism, racism would not go away or even decrease. Rather, Americans of all colors would lose treasured freedoms and opportunities. Forcing "equity" economically through the state would spark strife and discontent. Whatever legacy remains of slavery, Jim Crow, or redlining is best treated by the possibilities and opportunities afforded through free enterprise, rather than by insisting on compensatory will-o'-the-wisps notions, such as affirmative action, minimum wage laws, tax increases on "the rich," reparations, and other political dead ends. If any social system should be committed to the flames on the basis of evidence, principle, and history, it is socialism in all of its forms.

CHAPTER SEVEN

RACE AND IDENTITY

We hear much about *identity* today. Someone *identifies* as male or female or otherwise, irrespective of their biology. Some have even forged their identities for self-promotion. Rachel Dolezal, a woman who claimed to be black and was involved in black causes, made headlines in 2015 when she was outed by her white parents for being white. Undaunted, she said, "I identify as black." This did not go over well in the black community, and it raises the issue of the limits of reality on self-identification.[1]

Identity politics emphasizes treating people differently based on their race or gender. As such, it challenges the idea of a colorblind or gender-blind society—that is, treating people essentially as human beings who have the same equality, dignity, and rights as other human beings. Behind it, though, is the greatest question of all: how should human beings as a species be identified?

Image-Bearers of God

How we answer this question will determine our views of psychology, politics, education, economics, and culture. While CRT starts with race and gender as the ruling aspects of being human, the Christian vision of humanity starts elsewhere—with God, in the beginning. Human beings are not the result of impersonal and unguided forces of nature evolving over millions of years, but are, rather, created in the image and likeness of God. On the sixth day of creation:

> God said, "Let us make mankind in our image, in our likeness, so that they may rule over the fish in the sea and the birds in the sky, over the livestock and all the wild animals, and over all the creatures that move along the ground."
> So God created mankind in his own image,
> in the image of God he created them;
> male and female he created them.
> God blessed them and said to them, "Be fruitful and increase in number; fill the earth and subdue it. Rule over the fish in the sea and the birds in the sky and over every living creature that moves on the ground." (Genesis 1:26–28; see also 5:1–2; Psalm 8)

Whatever the disputes on the biological and historical meaning of race, the Bible teaches there is but *one human race*. Humans find their origin and identity in the creative act of a personal God.[2] Nor are human beings divine or emanations of God. We are finite and personal images of the infinite and personal God. Humans reflect and represent the agency, creativity, rationality, and relationality of their Creator. Our first parents were created with the purpose of marrying, procreating, and thriving in the creation of culture. Humans have a God-given dignity, nature, and purpose in His world. Human life is not to be taken through murder, since people bear God's image (Genesis 9:6; Exodus 20:13). Nor should anyone be libeled or slandered, given their status as image-bearers of God (Exodus 20:16; Matthew 5:21–23; James 3:9–10). Racial epithets and slurs are, therefore, condemned.

Created from One Man

When Paul preached to the philosophers on Mars Hill in Athens, he challenged his learned audience by claiming that God has made all people—including the Athenians listening to him—from one man.

> From one man he made all the nations, that they should inhabit the whole earth; and he marked out their appointed times in history and the boundaries of their lands. God did this so that they would seek him and perhaps reach out for him and find him, though he is not far from any one of us. (Acts 17:26–27)

The Athenians proudly traced their origin to their own Greek soil, from which they sprang unique and which made them superior to those of other races. This was ethnocentrism, if not racism. Yet Paul affirms the unity and equality of the human race. There is but one human race. All the nations—and thus all the peoples—of the world receive their objective value and purpose from their Maker.

One's fundamental identity is being made in the Divine Image; it is not found in race or gender or social class. Shelby Steele makes this point—without referring to the Bible—when he speaks of being half white and half black.

I never know what people really want to know when they ask me what it is like to be—and here come the math words—"biracial" or "multiracial" or "multicultural." The self as the answer to an addition problem.[3]

The *human* self is the answer, and every human self, though fallen, bears the Divine Image.

Equally Fallen into Sin

Our first parents, whatever color they may have been, listened to the deceiving serpent, turned against God, were expelled from the garden, and brought a curse upon creation (Genesis 3). Just as all human beings came from one man (Acts 17:26–27), so through that man sin and death came into the world (Romans 5:2). "All have sinned and fall short of the glory of God" (Romans 3:23).

This is a universal judgment on all races, all people, and throughout all history. The Bible knows nothing of any hierarchy of sinners by race or by any other innate quality. We all sin because we are all sinners, and we all need redemption through one God-man, Jesus Christ (1 Timothy 2:5).

> But the gift is not like the trespass. For if the many died by the trespass of the one man, how much more did God's grace and the gift that came by the grace of the one man, Jesus Christ, overflow to the many! (Romans 5:15)

Jesus commissioned His followers to take the Gospel to all people, as He told His disciples, "But you will receive power when the Holy Spirit comes on you; and you will be my witnesses in Jerusalem, and in all Judea and Samaria, and to the ends of the earth" (Acts 1:8; see also Matthew 28:18–20). But some have wrongly taught that the dark-skinned are under a special curse.

Ham, Race, and Truth

Over the centuries, many who have been invested in slavery have cited Genesis 9:20–27 to ground their view that the darker-skinned races were inferior and under an enduring curse, "the curse of Ham." James Baldwin speaks of this being used against him as a black man in his book *The Fire Next Time,*[4] and Kendi mentions it in *How to Be an Antiracist.*[5]

When Noah awoke from a drunken stupor to find that Ham had asked his brothers Shem and Japheth to cover his nakedness with a garment, Noah cursed Canaan (Ham's son), not Ham himself. The Canaanites later became the enemies of Israel and the recipients of God's judgment. However, there is no specific racial component involved, since all the parties were Semites.[6] Just how and when the races became differently pigmented is not addressed in the Bible, because skin color makes no difference whatsoever to God.[7] While the Bible refers to some people as having dark skin (such as Ethiopians; see Acts 8), it makes no reference to any having white skin, "and in no instance is the color black disparaged, nor any other color for that matter, nor is any color favored."[8] Jesus Christ, God Incarnate, demonstrates this truth.

Jesus, Two Women, and Race

Jesus often shocked his contemporaries by speaking to women, since this was not customary for a rabbi of his day.[9] But He doubly scandalized many when He spoke of women who were also of an ethnic group not valued by his fellow Jews. To use the popular CRT idea and term, these women were disadvantaged at the *intersection* of their gender and their race. For our purposes, I will emphasize race.

In John's gospel, we learn that Jesus had an extended conversation with an unnamed foreign woman (John 4:3–26). On his way to Galilee, Jesus stopped at Jacob's Well in Sychar, a town in Samaria. Fatigued from the journey, Jesus asks a woman if she would give Him a drink. The woman was stunned since she recognized him as a Jew, and Jews had nothing to do with Samaritans. The Jews held that Samaritans were "unclean." Jesus uses the opportunity to discuss His mission. "If you knew the gift of God and who it is that asks you for a drink, you would have asked Him and he would have given you living water." The woman wonders how Jesus could provide this, since He had nothing with which to draw the water. Jesus responds, "All who drink this water will be thirsty again, but those who drink the water I give them will never thirst. Indeed, the water I give them will become in them a spring of water welling up to eternal life."

The woman requests this water of Jesus, but Jesus says that she should call her husband and then come back. She replies that she has no husband. Jesus says that she has had five husbands and that the man she now has is not her husband. The woman, who must have been startled by the knowledge displayed by this Jewish stranger, declares that He is a prophet. She then says, "Our ancestors worshipped on this mountain, but you Jews claim that the place where we must worship is in Jerusalem." To this, Jesus offers a theological explanation and a prophecy.

> "Woman," Jesus replied, "believe me, a time is coming when you will worship the Father neither on this mountain nor in Jerusalem. You Samaritans worship what you do not know; we worship what we do know, for salvation is from the Jews. Yet a time is coming and has now come when the

true worshipers will worship the Father in the Spirit and in
truth, for they are the kind of worshipers the Father seeks.
God is spirit, and His worshipers must worship in the Spirit
and in truth." (John 4:21–24)

The woman returns the theological volley: "I know that Messiah
(called Christ) is coming. When he comes, he will explain everything
to us." Jesus then declares, "I who speak to you am He." This is the
only time in the gospels, prior to His trial and crucifixion (Matthew
26:62–65), when Jesus directly claims to be the Messiah. He says it
during a theological conversation with an outcast, a Samaritan woman.
It is no wonder that John tells us that "His disciples returned and were
surprised to find Him talking with a woman." The woman then went
to her town and proclaimed, "Come, see a man who told me everything
I ever did. Could this be the Christ?" At her urging, many Samaritans
came to Jesus. They convinced him to stay with them for two days,
during which they heard His teachings. Many became believers.

This tells us that a social outcast of the oppressed race and gender
was authorized by Jesus to tell others about Him.[10] The Christian
movement would continue to welcome women and those of various
racial backgrounds to be part of its fellowship and leadership (Acts
13:1–3: Galatians 3:26–28).

Jesus's interaction with another woman cannot be avoided in a
discussion of the Bible and race. It is an encounter Jesus had with a
desperate foreign woman.[11] When Jesus traveled to Tyre and Sidon,
He "entered a house and did not want anyone to know it; yet He
could not keep his presence secret" (Mark 7:24). Nevertheless, a
Greek woman, born in Syrophoenicia, implored Jesus, "crying out,
'Lord, Son of David, have mercy on me! My daughter is demon-
possessed and suffering terribly'" (Matthew 15:22). But, at first, Jesus
did not answer.

So his disciples came to Him and urged Him, "Send her away, for she keeps crying out after us." He answered, "I was sent only to the lost sheep of Israel." The woman came and knelt before Him. "Lord, help me!" she said. He replied, "It is not right to take the children's bread and toss it to the dogs." "Yes it is, Lord," she said. "Even the dogs eat the crumbs that fall from their master's table." Then Jesus said to her, "Woman, you have great faith! Your request is granted." And her daughter was healed at that moment. (Matthew 15:23–28)

Although Jesus miraculously answered this mother's earnest, persistent, and witty response, He initially paused, then refused, even using a derogatory name "dogs" for the racial group to which she and her daughter belonged. In these racially charged days, some have said Jesus's response was racist.

Jesus was sent primarily to His own people, the Jews, during His earthly ministry. In many cases, He did minister to non-Jews, as the Gospel of Luke emphasizes. During this event, He was in a largely non-Jewish area. Jesus denied that salvation was limited to the Jews (Luke 13:29), but He affirmed that salvation was "from the Jews" (John 4:22). Paul says this as well, "For I am not ashamed of the gospel, because it is the power of God that brings salvation to everyone who believes: first to the Jew, then to the Gentile" (Romans 1:16). So, the Jewish priority principle applies here.

Note that Jesus, unlike His disciples, did not tell the woman to go away. He first paused. By pausing to answer, Jesus allowed His disciples' antipathy to non-Jews to be exposed. He was baiting them to reveal their bias and setting up the situation for this non-Jewish woman to reveal her "great faith" (Matthew 15:28).[12] If Jesus had been a racist, He would not have commended the woman's faith or healed her daughter. By pausing and challenging the woman, He drew out her faith through sacred repartee. It is highly unlikely that any other person could have engaged the situation in this way without sinning, but Jesus had a supernatural insight into people's souls and acted accordingly (John 2:23–25).

Christianity and Interracial Marriage

Unfortunately, despite the biblical teaching of racial equality, some American Christians have opposed interracial marriage, particularly between blacks and whites. It was not until June 12, 1967, that the Supreme Court unanimously ruled that laws prohibiting interracial marriage—then called *miscegenation*—violated the Fourteenth Amendment to the Constitution (guaranteeing equal protection under the law) and were nullified. The case had been brought by Richard (white) and Mildred Loving (black and native American), represented by the ACLU, who had been arrested in Virginia in 1958 for the crime of being married. They had married in Washington, D.C., where it was legal. At the time of the ruling in 1967, sixteen states disallowed interracial marriage.[13]

Since there is but one human race and because differences in skin color are ontologically and morally irrelevant before God, there is no biblical reason to prohibit interracial marriage.[14] Any theological justifications offered to prohibit or condemn intermarriage are rooted ultimately in racial superiority and thus in spurious concepts and abused texts.[15] The idea of "racial purity" has no standing in Scripture, although the ideas "moral purity" and "doctrinal purity" do. When God told the Old Testament Israelites not to marry those from other nations, the prohibition was based on culture and religion, not on race (Deuteronomy 7:3-4; 1 Kings 11:1-43; Nehemiah 10:1-30). The biblical norm is one man and one woman united in love by covenant and under God (Genesis 2: 18-25; Matthew 19:1-6; 1 Timothy 3:2). Moreover, as black pastor and civil rights activist C. Herbert Oliver wrote about the creation mandate, "[W]hen God commanded men to replenish the earth, He did not divide men into racial camps and tell them to replenish the earth with their own race. He gave men dominion over the animals, but not over each other."[16]

Americans' attitudes toward interracial marriage have changed radically for the better in recent decades, and this is evidence against the change that America is systemically racist. President Barack Obama was the son of a black father and a white mother. The Pew Research Center reports that

> In 1967, when miscegenation laws were overturned in the United States, 3% of all newlyweds were married to someone of a different race or ethnicity. Since then, inter-marriage rates have steadily climbed. By 1980, the share of intermarried newlyweds had about doubled to 7%. And by 2015 the number had risen to 17%.[17]

While "intermarriage" refers to more than black and white marriages, the study notes that increases in intermarriage stem "in part [from] rising intermarriage rates among black newlyweds and among white newlyweds. The share of recently married blacks with a spouse of a different race or ethnicity has more than tripled, from 5% in 1980 to 18% in 2015."[18]

Attitudes, not surprisingly, have changed radically as well. Summarizing the data, Pew Research claims in 2017 that "A growing share of adults say that the trend toward more people of different races marrying each other is generally a good thing for American society." The "share saying they would oppose a close relative marrying someone of a different race has fallen dramatically."[19] Nearly one in four people say interracial marriage is "good for society," 52 percent says "it doesn't make much of a difference," and only 9 percent say it is a "bad thing."[20] For these changes, we should be grateful, since God does not limit our love by race, but only by his standards and his guidance.[21]

No White Man's Religion

Charges to the contrary, Christianity is no "white man's religion," nor is it uniquely Western in its history.[22] A warped version of Christianity was used by some white people to enslave black people, but it is not a religion for white people and against black people. Listen to Frederick Douglass.

> What I have said respecting and against religion, I mean strictly to apply to the slaveholding religion of this land, and with no possible reference to Christianity proper; for, between the Christianity of this land, and the Christianity of Christ, I recognize the widest possible difference—so wide, that to receive the one as good, pure, and holy, is of necessity to reject the other as bad, corrupt, and wicked. To be the friend of the one, is of necessity to be the enemy of the other. I love the pure, peaceable, and impartial Christianity of Christ: I therefore hate the corrupt, slave-holding, women-whipping, cradle-plundering, partial and hypocritical Christianity of this land.[23]

At its inception, Christianity spread in several directions, encompassing many peoples over time. It came to India, possibly through the Apostle Thomas. There is evidence for Christianity in ancient China as well. Philip Jenkins explores this profitably in *The Lost History of Christianity*.[24]

Far from essentially being a religion imposed by white people on others, Christianity was multinational and multiracial from the start. While it is often assumed that white and Western Christianity came to non-Western nations in the wake of colonialism, this is too simple. Missionaries often did not rely on colonial powers.[25] Nothing in the Bible supports spreading the faith through any political coercion. Christianity today is growing the fastest in the two-thirds world, which is nonwhite, as Jenkins documents in *The Next Christendom*.[26]

Church History in Living Color

Historian Ruth Tucker wrote a provocative essay called "Colorizing Church History: A History That Ignores Women and Minorities Is a Poor Reflection of Our Christian Heritage." Without challenging the notions of objective truth, rationality, or the need for impartial evidence, Tucker asks why our accounts of church history are dominated by white men when, in fact, God has powerfully used women and people of other races to propagate, defend, and apply the Gospel through the centuries.

She notes that God often uses the weak and small things of the world for great purposes (Matthew 20:26; 1 Corinthians 1:27–28). Thus, Christians should recognize that "a history that focuses on those with prestige and position is not the fullest reflection of our Christian heritage—in that it is out of step with how God works in the world."[27]

Our understanding of church history influences our views of ourselves and others. We are historical beings who need heroes to emulate (Hebrews 11). Those struggling for recognition and opportunity need strong role models for inspiration. "The standard list of great nineteenth-century American revivalists invariably leaves off men and women of color."[28] We hear much of Charles Finney's

(1792–1875) influence but little of John Jasper (1812–1901), his African American contemporary. Both ministered for over half a century and were recognized as powerful preachers who drew enthusiastic crowds. Jasper began a church in Richmond, Virginia, with nine members, which grew to over two thousand. Although he was a "great humanitarian and defender of the Bible…his story has been lost in obscurity.[29]

Samson Occom (1723–92) was a preacher and evangelist who ministered for over forty years in eighteenth-century New England and New York. He studied at a school that later became Dartmouth, ministered in England, and published a hymnal for his people.[30] Why is he omitted from Sydney Ahlstrom's well-respected work *A Religious History of the American People*? Occom was a Mohegan Indian.[31]

Tucker issues a clarion challenge:

> We need to re-examine the lens we use to view church history. Like the writers of Scripture, we need to focus on the significance of women, minorities, and those of various cultures. Only by using this more inclusive lens will we have any hope of seeing the full spectacle of what God is accomplishing on earth through his church—and any hope of seeing him, and each other, more clearly.[32]

Tucker does not advocate a quota system for church history or a compensatory model that vilifies previous heroes (typically white males) to make room for new (nonwhite) ones. Rather, "Church history must be told anew—not to satisfy certain interest groups, but to capture the whole picture of the church and to listen to voices that have traditionally not been heard."[33] Yes indeed, but what of our images of Jesus?

Whitewashing Christianity?

Images of Jesus affect our sense of God and salvation in many ways—even if the *written word* about Jesus in the Bible should matter far more. Many depictions of Jesus in the West are surely untrue to the appearance of a Jew in the first century. Jesus did not have brown hair and lily-white skin. That would be a whitewashed Jesus. Noted black preacher E. V. Hill (1933–2003) got to the heart of the matter.

> I don't know anything about a white Christ—I know about Christ, a Savior, named Jesus! I don't know what color He is. He was born in brown Asia, He fled to black Africa, and He was in heaven before the gospel got to white Europe, so I don't know what color He is. I do know one thing, if you bow at the altar with color on your mind, and get up with color on your mind, go back again—and keep going back until you no longer look at His color, but at His greatness and His power—His power to save![34]

This was Pastor Hill's response to the violent Black Panthers, who said he was preaching "a white Jesus" and that if he didn't preach "a black Jesus," they would murder him in his church the next Sunday. Hill, a man of great courage, had also been threatened by the Ku Klux Klan. He must be one of the only people to ever be threatened with death by both white supremacists and black nationalists. However, he died a peaceful death at age sixty-nine, having been protected by his Savior.[35]

Sadly, American culture has often been whitewashed as well because African Americans have not been fairly represented or invited into all of culture. This violates the biblical injunction to not show favoritism based on social status. "My brothers and sisters, believers in our glorious Lord Jesus Christ must not show favoritism" (James 2:1).

This exclusion has not been as bad in much of music (classical music is an exception) or many sports, but black people have been excluded in other areas, such as, until recent decades, films and television. Hattie McDaniel was the first black actor or actress to receive an Academy award in 1940 for best supporting actress in *Gone with the Wind* (1939) in which she played Mammy. She accepted her award in a segregated hotel, and said through tears, "I sincerely hope that I shall always be a credit to my race and the motion picture industry. My heart is too full to tell you how I feel."[36]

Actors such as Sidney Poitier (1927–2022) bravely won respect for black people in critically acclaimed and popular films that addressed controversial aspects of black life in America. These include 1961's *A Raisin in the Sun* (segregation), *In the Heat of the Night,* (prejudice against a black professional), and *Guess Who's Coming to Dinner?* (interracial marriage), both released in 1967. Poitier rightly won the Presidential Medal of Freedom in 2009.[37]

Christians should see to it that honor is given to whom honor is due, whatever that person's age, race, ethnicity, or gender. As Proverbs teaches: "Do not withhold good from those to whom it is due, when it is in your power to act" (Proverbs 3:27). The alternative is simply sin: "If you really keep the royal law found in Scripture, 'Love your neighbor as yourself,' you are doing right. But if you show favoritism, you sin and are convicted by the law as lawbreakers" (James 2:8–9).

Reading the Bible with People of Color

In the last twenty-five years or so, many biblical scholars, theologians, and others have considered how one's racial and ethnic identity and context affects how one reads the Bible.[38] The Bible is not a collection of books to be morphed into whatever shape we want—because it has a determinative meaning—but those of different races and with different experiences may discern objective truths that others have not.[39] The Bible is for everyone—men and women of all colors; old and young; rich, poor, and in-the-middle (2 Timothy 3:15–17). It speaks to our condition, whatever our condition. God spoke through it even to black people whose masters misused it to enslave them, and we find record of this in the spirituals.[40]

Much of Christian theology has been written and taught by white males. That, in itself, does not make it wrong or questionable. But we all have blind spots, and some are enormous. For example, several American theologians owned slaves and/or supported slavery. Some supported the South in the Civil War. That is no small thing, and any vestige of racism needs to be purged from our theology and institutional identities.[41]

Any eager and gifted student of Scripture should be taken seriously. For example, the *Africa Bible Commentary* contains insights from native African scholars and is instructive for those outside—and inside—that setting.[42] I often use it in preparing sermons. Recently, Esau McCaulley, a young black New Testament scholar, has written *Reading While Black: African American Biblical Interpretation as an Exercise of Hope*, in which he attends to "black ecclesial interpretation" of Scripture.[43] This perspective opens up new questions and suggests new insights into the Bible, such as what Romans 13:1–7 might tell about a theology of policing wherein those who are innocent can feel safe and not harassed by racial profiling.[44] One need not appeal to black liberation theology (James Cone)[45] to derive these insights, since solidly biblical writers are doing this work.[46]

Glenn Loury is an African-American economist and writer, who has widely criticized CRT in recent years. His proclamation of his identity hits all the right notes and summarizes this chapter well.

Who am I, then? Foremost, I am a child of God, created in his image, imbued with his spirit, endowed with his gifts, set free by his grace. The most important challenges and opportunities that confront me derive not from my racial condition, but rather from my human condition. I am a husband, a father, a son, a teacher, an intellectual, a Christian, a citizen. In none of these roles is my race irrelevant, but neither can racial identity alone provide much guidance for my quest to discharge these responsibilities adequately.[47]

SECTION IV

A BETTER FIRE

CHAPTER EIGHT

A CHRISTIAN FRAMEWORK

"The reason I was born and came into the world
is to testify to the truth. Everyone on the side of truth
listens to me."

—*Jesus Christ (John 8:37)*

Throughout this book, I have critiqued CRT from a biblical world-view. I hope this vantage point has given realism and muscle to it, but in this chapter, I give a constructive defense of Christianity as true, rational, and pertinent to matters raised by CRT. I have offered a thorough defense of Christianity elsewhere,[1] but here I will focus on the inability of atheism to counter CRT, the scientific evidence for God's existence, and the Christian account of human nature as grounding wise civil government. But before giving a constructive account of Christianity, we need to size up another critique of CRT.

A Misbegotten Critique of CRT: Atheism

Over twenty years ago, I wrote of the confluence of secular critics and Christians who both rejected postmodernism's denial of objective truth and normative rationality. The secularists who deemed science as the greatest of intellectual achievements blanched when postmodernists tried to deconstruct science into simply one perspective among many, or one kind of discourse in a sea of possible interpretations of reality. Christians agreed that there was an objective reality (as created by God) that could be known through the proper methods. The difference came in what that reality was taken to be. Secularists, such as biologist Edmund O. Wilson and philosopher John Searle, claimed that philosophical materialism fit the bill.[2] The objective truth was that God did not exist, and science told us so. Forget about constructing reality through language and all the rest. Science wins. God loses.

In *Cynical Theories*, Helen Pluckrose and James Lindsay give a cogent critique of CRT as illogical and ill-fitting a free society. They are classical liberals who rightly affirm that (1) objective truth is knowable through reason and evidence (as opposed to CRT's standpoint epistemology), that (2) individuals have moral value and human rights as opposed to making group identities based on gender and race definitive (as does CRT), and that (3) insuring and protecting free speech is better than silencing people based on the mistaken CRT ideology. However, like their likeminded colleagues, linguist Steven Pinker and philosopher Paul Boghossian, they are atheists. And there's the rub. Their worldview cannot support statements (1)–(3) above. However, a Christian worldview can.

The classical liberalism they affirm is rooted in the Judeo-Christian worldview and makes little sense without it. But in their view, humankind can only be understood by *looking back* at our evolutionary history. They believe we are nothing but evolved animals who got where we are by acting successfully on urges to survive. Our human nature is not the result of divine and intelligent design, they say, but of contingent material factors and natural laws. Evolution selects for reproductive success, not for knowledge, virtue, or moral progress. As Pinker has written, "our brains were shaped for fitness, not for truth."[3] (And that is the truth, according to Pinker.) For these atheists, the human mind is supposed to have access to objective reality and to the kind of moral knowledge as mentioned above—but individuals possessing moral value and free speech is better than silencing people. If one believes that humans are created in the rational-moral image of God (Genesis 1:26) and live in a truth-conducive cosmos (John 1:1–5), then these claims are rationally supported. However, the atheist-materialist worldview provides no philosophical support for such august ideas. In order to affirm them, it must steal goods from the Judeo-Christian metaphysical storehouse. And theft is wrong.

The atheist-materialist cannot *look up* to our Creator God, who has designed us in order to know who we are and to live in a particular way for our own good, the good of others, and for God's honor. For them, there is no revelation from God in the Bible, in nature, or in conscience. We find in ourselves a welter of conflicting urges, and we are among others who also find in themselves a welter of conflicting urges. If there is no transcendent moral standard, then there is no way to discern which urges to follow and which to ignore. If Pinker and others are correct, this is because we are merely material beings shaped by instinct and external conditions. No instinct can judge other instincts; you need a standard outside of them, the conscience. C. S. Lewis speaks of hearing a cry from a man in danger and feeling both the desire to help and the desire to avoid danger yourself.

> But you will find inside you, in addition to these two impulses, a third thing which tells you that you ought to follow the impulse to help, and suppress the impulse to run away. Now this thing that judges between two instincts, that decides which should be encouraged, cannot itself be either of them. You might as well say that the sheet of music which tells you, at a given moment, to play one note on the

piano and not another, is itself one of the notes on the keyboard. The Moral Law tells us the tune we have to play: our instincts are merely the keys.[4]

According to atheism-materialism, there is no objective moral law impinging on and obligating individuals and societies. In other words, materialism cannot provide a moral standpoint from which to evaluate individuals and cultures. As C. S. Lewis put it, those who deny "the doctrine of objective value" are "trying to get a conclusion in the imperative mood out of premises in the indicative mood: and though he continues trying through all eternity he cannot succeed, for the thing is impossible."[5] It is one thing to describe a state of affairs (the indicative mood); it is quite another to prescribe what states of affairs are good and which are not good (the imperative mood).

Atheism-materialism grants human beings no privileged access to reality (moral or otherwise), nor does it give human beings a uniquely important moral standing in nature or society. Human animals simply happened to come out on top after a long and undirected evolutionary process. If human beings have no objective moral value, then there is no reason to grant them the freedom of speech or any objective moral rights. Human relationships in society reduce to power relationships—instinct against instinct, person against person, group against group. Arthur Leff concluded that without God, the prospects for morality are bleak indeed.

> All I can say is this: it looks as if we are all we have. Given what we know about ourselves and each other, this is an extraordinarily unappetizing prospect; looking around the world, it appears that if all men are brothers, the ruling model is Cain and Abel. Neither reason, nor love, nor even terror, seems to have worked to make us "good," and

worse than that, there is no reason why anything should. Only if ethics were something unspeakable by us, could law be unnatural, and therefore unchallengeable. As things now stand, everything is up for grabs.[6]

Nevertheless, Leff concludes his brilliant essay by affirming objective moral truths that we all know (such as "napalming babies is wrong")—in total contradiction of his entire argument. Such is the terminal doublemindedness of moralistic atheism. But there is a better way.

Truth in God's World

Let us return to the three claims made above, all of which contradict CRT thinking: (1) Objective truth is knowable through reason and evidence, (2) individuals have moral value and human rights as opposed to making group identities based on gender and race definitive, and (3) insuring and protecting free speech is better than silencing people. These claims are part of the Western tradition of what has been called *classical liberalism*—which is not the same as modern liberalism or leftism. This view is steeped in the Judeo-Christian worldview, although some claim its provenance traces to the Enlightenment. Inasmuch as the Enlightenment influence is atheistic, this claim is unsupportable.[7]

Neither the CRT view nor the atheist-materialist view examined above can make room for the claim that (1) objective truth is knowable through reason and evidence. We have already discussed CRT's dilemma of claiming its view is objectively true while denying that objective truth exists. Moreover, if all our perceptions are determined by race and gender, objectivity is unobtainable. However, a Christian worldview offers an account of truth that is rational and meaningful, and which makes knowable possible.

Christianity does not offer a unique understanding of truth (although it offers a unique set of truth claims), but it assumes the correspondence view of truth, as have most major Western philosophers. A statement (or truth claim) is true if, and only if, it corresponds to reality.[8] Truth is not determined by a majority, by ethnicity, or by any perspective. Facts makes statements true. "Alaska is the forty-ninth state of the union" is true. A statement is false if it fails to correspond to reality. "Alaska is the fiftieth state of the union" is false. This is the commonsense account of truth, which we assume in all our conservations, questions, and arguments.

Inasmuch as CRT denies the correspondence view, it becomes incoherent, since it presents itself as true and worthy of belief. It takes non-CRT views to be false and unworthy of belief. Christianity assumes the correspondence view and makes many truth claims, such as "Jesus is Lord." More than that, the Christian view of truth is paired with a compelling account of how we come to know truth. A person knows a statement to be true if she (1) believes that statement, (2) that statement is true, and (3) there is adequate evidence or support for that belief. Knowledge is thus justified and true belief.[9]

I have argued that the materialist-atheist worldview does not allow for objective knowledge, since mindless evolution could not have had knowledge in mind for our merely material brains. Folks like Pluckrose and Lindsay want to preserve objective truth, human rights, and free speech within their inadequate worldview. CRT advocates, on the other hand, may or may not be theists, but they collapse knowledge into racial and gendered perspectives and even claim that rationality is thus conditioned. If so, we lose any hopes of adjudicating truth claims through appeals to reason and evidence. There could be no public square for rational discussion. But Christianity offers a better way.

According to the Bible, human beings are all made in the image and likeness of a personal and communicative God. God created us, body and soul, to represent Him in the world and to develop creation through our abilities. I mentioned this account in another chapter, but here I want to concentrate on rationality and evidence. John's gospel tells us that:

> In the beginning was the Word, and the Word was with God, and the Word was God. He was with God in the beginning. Through him all things were made; without him nothing was made that has been made. In him was life, and that life was the light of all mankind. (John 1:1–4)

This language is quite similar to Genesis 1:1: "In the beginning, God created the heavens and the earth." However, John adds that the Word was with God and was God. The Greek word for "Word" is *logos,* from whence we get our English word logic. We are later told that "the Word became flesh," which refers to Jesus of Nazareth as God incarnate (1:14). Although we could discuss the significance of the divine Word being "with God"—a reference to God the Son and God the Father—we will rather expand on this concept of Logos.

For the Greek philosophers of the day, Logos was generally an impersonal ordering principle that gave coherence and meaning to the cosmos. So, John drops a bombshell on the philosophical playground by *personalizing* the Logos, who was God, who was with God, who created all things, and who became a human being in Jesus. However, the concept of rationality or reason remains. This Word is rational and gives a rational ordering to all His creation. Further, He gives "light" to "all mankind." According to theologian Carl F. H. Henry, the

Logos of God grounded the meaning and purpose of man and the world, and objective reality was held to be divinely structured by complex formal patterns. Endowed with more than animal perception, gifted in fact with a mode of cognition not to be confused with sensation, man was therefore able to intuit intelligible universals; as a divinely intended knower, he was able to cognize, within limits, the nature and structure of the externally real world.[10]

Human beings, made in the image of a rational and personal God (Logos), are thus equipped to know the world aright. Henry says humans can "intuit intelligible universals." As Schaeffer says, "The personal-infinite God who has made the world and has put me into it...[made] the categories of mind to fit the place where he put me."[11] We need not be imprisoned by racial or gender categories in our knowing.

Everyone should know, for example, that the law of noncontradiction is true—at least if they think about it for a moment. Nothing can possess incompatible properties. A woman cannot both have and not have African ancestry, for example. It is an either/or. This universal truth can be intuited by all people, since all people are made in God's image and because the Logos is "the light of all mankind." Or as the Psalmist said, echoing John, "For with you is the fountain of life; in your light we see light" (Psalm 36:9).

Because of this knowledge-friendly worldview, the Bible repeatedly makes truth claims that are testable and knowable, particularly about history and morality. The Apostle Peter reports that "we did not follow cleverly devised stories when we told you about the coming of our Lord Jesus Christ in power, but we were eyewitnesses of his majesty" (2 Peter 1:16). When God gave the Ten Commandments, He did so publicly and obviously, so as to leave no room for doubt (Exodus 19–20).

Please do not think I am getting too technical. Nothing less than the knowledge of reality is at stake in controversies over CRT. This concerns who we are as human beings and how we all ought to be treated as God's image-bearers.

The Return of God in Science

If we want a good explanation for the origin and nature of our rational abilities and how they relate to the objective world, then Christianity provides it. That in itself gives credence to Christianity, even apart from the abundant evidence for the existence of God from science and philosophy. The Christian emphasis on an orderly and knowable universe contributed decisively to the development of modern science, as documented by philosopher of science Stephen C. Meyer in his book *Return of the God Hypothesis*. Meyer's account is clear, convincing, and incorporates new insights from science and philosophy. Modern scientists spoke of three controlling metaphors inspired by the Bible that spurred scientific discovery. First, nature is God's *book* to be read through scientific investigation. Second, nature is God's *clockwork mechanism* that works in an orderly way. Third, God's world is controlled by *objective laws*, which explain its orderly operation.

The Christian account of nature led to the scientific revolution and helped imprint principles of inquiry on the Western mind. Scientists such as Blaise Pascal, Michael Faraday, Johannes Kepler, Galileo, and others prized empirical observation and rational analysis to unlock the secrets of nature. CRT deconstructs this model in favor of standpoint epistemology, which privileges the perspectives of POC and sexual minorities. But the vision that motivated the scientific revolution makes for a better method of discovery, given its emphasis on objective truth and the power of observation and rationality.

Meyer also presents scientific arguments for God's existence, all
of which have gained power in recent decades through cutting-edge
discoveries. Far from banishing God from the universe, modern science confirms God's existence in three main areas: the origin of the
universe, the design of the universe as a whole, and the origin of life
on earth.[12]

Meyer explains the development of "the Big Bang theory" of
cosmology, which starts with Albert Einstein's general theory of rela-
tivity (1915). This predicted an expanding universe, which was verified
through scientific discoveries. Further evidence led scientists to affirm
an absolute beginning for the universe out of nothing. The case has
not weakened over time and has remained compelling, even through
several challenges. The upshot is that the cosmos was created.

Meyer further argues that the fine-tuning of the universe is best
explained by a Mind. We live in "the Goldilocks universe," which is
constituted to be "just right" for life. "The most fundamental type of
fine tuning pertains to the laws of physics and chemistry."[13] There are
dozens of variables in the universe that are required for life. Each
variable has multiple possible values, and each of them must be bal-
anced on a razor's edge to make life an option. These contingent
features are called "anthropic coincidences" and have only become
known in the last fifty years or so. The odds are astronomically
against these variables having life-permitting values by mere chance,
since a dead universe is (statistically speaking) far, far more likely. A
Mind that designed the world is the far better explanation. But this
Mind had something else in mind: biology.

The information in DNA cannot be accounted for by merely natural
processes, and all naturalistic attempts have failed. Any time we find
information in the world—whether in a book or in skywriting or anywhere else—we infer an intelligent author or designer is behind it. Thus,
based on what Meyer calls "our reliable and uniform experience," when

we find a specified function for communication, we justifiably infer design. On this basis, Meyer finds compelling evidence for an intelligent designer behind the highly complex and specified system of DNA. Moreover, the kind of intelligence found in DNA could not have been front-loaded into the Big Bang. New information had to be added to the preexisting mix by a divine mind.

God's Image, the Fall, and Civil Government

We have presented a biblical case for the existence and know-ability of truth—over against atheism-materialism—and given evidence for the existence of a creator-designer God from science. As such, we have a firm foundation to investigate the specifically Christian understanding of human nature in relation to civil government. An account of human nature is needed for a coherent view of human culture and politics, since it is human beings who live, work, play, dream, and die together. To know how we ought to live together, we need to know who we are: where we came from, what is conducive to human flourishing, and what social arrangements to avoid. Christianity teaches that God created human beings in His rational-moral image, placed them in a truth-conducive world, and charged them to procreate and develop nature into culture.

But the next act in the story tells us that our first parents foolishly denied God's authority, listened to the deceiver, did the one thing God told them not to do, and suffered the consequences by being expelled from the garden to live in a world of sweat, pain, and tears; we now live in a world full of mixed motives, selfish urges, and hurtful ways (Genesis 3; Romans 3; Mark 7:21-23)—all of which we are aware since our conscience bears witness to this moral law (Romans 2:14–15). While other religions and philosophers may tell of some primeval disturbance that brought woe upon the world—think of

Pandora's Box—no other religion or philosophy paints the picture as clearly or starkly.[14]

The evidence of the Fall is evident within us and without us; as G. K. Chesterton reports, "Certain new theologians dispute original sin, which is the only part of Christian theology which can really be proved."[15] Hyperbole aside, the point stands. Human corruption is epidemic and rampant. Look in the mirror. Look at the internet. Read history.

The doctrine of the Fall, while not without mystery, explains us to ourselves. As Pascal noted about the idea of original sin: "For without it, what are we to say man is? His whole state depends on this imperceptible point."

> Certainly nothing jolts us more rudely than this doctrine, and yet, but for this mystery, the most incomprehensible of all, we remain incomprehensible to ourselves. The knot of our condition was twisted and turned in that abyss, so that it is harder to conceive of man without this mystery than for man to conceive of it himself.[16]

The doctrine of original sin is the great leveler, as Chesterton saw. Original sin, he says,

> may also be described as the doctrine of the equality of men. But the essential point of it is merely this, that whatever primary and far-reaching moral dangers affect any man, affect all men. All men can be criminals, if tempted; all men can be heroes, if inspired.[17]

While original sin is the original tragedy, it teaches us who we are and how we ought to live as fallen people in a broken world

(Romans 8:16–24). As Jesus said, "It is not the healthy who need a doctor, but the sick. I have not come to call the righteous, but sinners" (Mark 2:17). Those who know they are sinners—who are weighed down by true moral guilt against God—can find redemption through a Savior. As Jesus also proclaimed, "I want you to know that the Son of Man has authority on earth to forgive sins" (Mark 2:10). The biblical view of sin and salvation is good news for our philosophy of civil government. Let us consider the human condition as it pertains to our lives together.

Blaise Pascal, a leading early modern scientist, reflected philosophically on the human condition.

> Man's greatness and wretchedness are so evident that the true religion must necessarily teach us that there is in man some great principle of greatness and some great principle of wretchedness. It must also account for such amazing contradictions.[18]

The principle of greatness is the Divine Image. The principle of wretchedness is the Fall. We are not "dust in the wind," nor are we gods. We are, rather, deposed kings. After writing of the distinctively human foibles, follies, and worse, Pascal observes: "All these examples of wretchedness prove his greatness. It is the wretchedness of a great lord, the wretchedness of a dispossessed king."[19] As deposed royalty, we retain a sense of our greatness, but always with an equal sense of our corruption.

Mere mortals can delve into the heart of nature and capture its treasures for human welfare and progress. Mere mortals can also treat each other like dirt, hurl racial epithets, and brag about it. What might this account of the human condition tell us about civil government?

Freedom of Conscience and Religion

Given all the press about the repressive nature of Christianity through the centuries, it may surprise some that Christianity was the first religion to develop a strong sense of the freedom of conscience and freedom of religion. Robert Louis Wilken, a noted historian of the Church, writes that early Christian thinkers, such as Tertullian and Lactantius, defended religious freedom as part of their apologetic that Christians could be good citizens, and should thus not be forced to violate their conscience in worshipping Caesar or any other god. In his *Apology*, Tertullian (AD 160–220) wrote:

> See that you do not end up fostering irreligion by taking away freedom of religion [*libertas religionis*] and forbid free choice with respect to divine matters, so that I am not allowed to worship what I wish, but am forced to worship what I do not wish. Not even a human being would like to be honored unwillingly.[20]

Wilken notes that "Tertullian is the first in the history of Western civilization to use the phrase 'freedom of religion.'"[21] Similarly, the theologian Lactantius (AD 240–320) wrote in *The Divine Institutes* that "religion cannot be imposed by force [*religio cogi non potest*]." Our will can only be moved "by words, not by blows."[22]

Thomas Jefferson was influenced by the Judeo-Christian view when he wrote that "we are endowed by our Creator with certain unalienable rights," which include "life, liberty, and the pursuit of happiness." The First Amendment was likewise influenced by this perspective when it ensured the freedom of religion, speech, press, and peaceful assembly.

These thinkers learned from Jesus and His apostles. There has never been a more compelling teacher or preacher than Jesus Christ, but He never compelled anyone through force or intimidation. His sole means for influence was persuasion through word, creed, and deed. Some believed and followed Him. Others refused. Still, He never threatened or cajoled anyone. Neither did the Apostles. The Book of Acts tells us that Peter preached primarily to the Jews that Jesus was the Messiah (Acts 2:14–41; etc.). Paul preached primarily to the Gentiles that Jesus was the Messiah, and he commanded their allegiance (Acts 17:16–34; etc.).[23] They, too, used only persuasion through word, creed, and deed. The answer to original sin was a supernatural Savior, Jesus Christ—crucified, buried, resurrected, ascended, enthroned, and coming again.

Of course, after the church began to acquire power in the Roman Empire under Constantine (who made Christianity legal), it often through the centuries used that power in ways inimical to its founder and His holy apostles. Yet no religion should be judged by its defections from its founding principles. Jesus predicted that many would come in His name, but not act according to His teachings (Matthew 7:15–27; 24:4–5).[24]

Universal Human Rights

Those who affirm and endorse universal human rights need a foundation on which to stand and a philosophy in which to believe. Sadly, CRT advocates do not make this claim, to their own detriment. For them, race and gender are more determinative of persons and rights than any universal realities based on human nature as such "under God." The Judeo-Christian worldview grants humans special status in the world, given their identity as beings uniquely made in God's image. But without that doctrine, humanity is imperiled philosophically and politically, as Francis Schaeffer and former U.S. Surgeon General C. Everett Koop (1982–89) argued in 1979:

If man is not made in the image of God, nothing then stands in the way of inhumanity. There is no good reason why mankind should be perceived as special. Human life is cheapened. We can see this in many of the major issues being debated in our society today: abortion, infanticide, euthanasia, the increase of child abuse and violence of all kinds, pornography (and its particular kinds of violence as evidenced in sadomasochism), the routine torture of political prisoners in many parts of the world, the crime explosion, and the random violence which surrounds us.[25]

But can human dignity be preserved without this biblical doctrine? Article 1 of the United Nations Declaration of Human Rights (1948) affirms this:

All human beings are born free and equal in dignity and rights. They are endowed with reason and conscience and should act towards one another in a spirit of brotherhood.[26]

This statement is objectively true, but what *makes it true*? Put another way, what else must be true about the world for this statement to be true—for it to rightly reflect reality? In biological terms, human beings are not born equal in their abilities or potentials. Some are stronger than others. Some are smarter than others. Some are more attractive than others. Some are born into poverty. Some are born into wealth. On that basis, social Darwinism is acceptable—nature *and culture* are "red in tooth and claw" (Tennyson). The survival of the fittest is the best we can do. To ground equality in "freedom and dignity" for human beings, we must appeal to something other than physical characteristics or social convention. In his bestselling book, *Sapiens*, Yuval Noah Harari admits that on his naturalistic-evolutionary account of homo sapiens (humans), he cannot ground a concept of universal justice for all people. Harari writes clearly what many refuse to admit:

> The Americans got the idea of equality from Christianity, which argues that every person has a divinely created soul, and that all souls are equal before God. However, if we do not believe in the Christian myths about God, creation and souls, what does it mean that all people are "equal"? Evolution is based on difference, not on equality. Every person carries a somewhat different genetic code, and is exposed from birth to different environmental influences. This leads to the development of different qualities that carry with them different chances of survival. "Created equal" should therefore be translated into "evolved differently."[27]

For there to be intrinsic human rights, there must be a common and essential feature of humanity that all humans share equally and which cannot be taken away by any human. It is, of course, the image of God.

As I argued above, mindless and material nature could not "endow" us with reason, since that requires a Reasoner (the Logos). Jefferson knew this when he wrote in the Declaration that "We are endowed by our Creator with certain unalienable rights . . ." Nor could mindless nature endow us with a conscience that answers to universal truths such as those propounded in this august declaration. And, finally, it is only the fatherhood of God that creates the brotherhood of men and women (Malachi 2:10; Acts 17:26). As Leff said (quoted above), "it appears that if all men are brothers, the ruling model is Cain and Abel." That is true enough, unless Jesus is our elder brother (Hebrews 2:11; Romans 8:29; Mark 3:34). If so, we have a hope that will not disappoint us (Romans 5:5).

The City of God and the City of Man

Christianity has contributed immeasurably to human progress regarding the development of science, religious freedom, and the recognition of universal human rights. Christians have been influential in opposing slavery, building the university, giving women the vote, and much more. But, of course, the track record is flawed, since Christians have often failed to advance these and other good causes. As disappointing and shameful as this is, the Bible never predicts that a perfectly just and harmonious society will emerge through merely human effort, or even through the ardent efforts of those who look to God for wisdom and strength. Jesus said that "the gates of hell would not prevail" against the Church (Matthew 16:18), but the government would be on His shoulder (Isaiah 9:6); and He will carry it through the vicissitudes of history and into eternity (1 Corinthians 15:20–28). The final redemption and judgment of the nations ("the kingdom" fully come) awaits a supernatural fulfillment at the Second Coming of Jesus. Before then, there will be no utopia and many dystopias.

Saint Augustine (AD 354–430) pondered the relationship of "the city of man" and "the city of God" in his massive work, *The City of God*. No summary of his seminal book is possible, but one controlling concept may help us navigate the political, racial, and gender strife of our day. The city of God is the unfolding of God's Kingdom in history and is animated by love. The city of man has other wellsprings. Both will exist side by side until the end, when the city of God descends from Heaven in the new heavens and the new Earth (Revelation 21–22). Augustine writes:

We see then that the two cities were created by two kinds of love: the earthly city was created by self-love reaching the point of contempt for God, the Heavenly City by the love of God carried as far as contempt of self. In fact, the earthly city glories in itself, the Heavenly City glories in the Lord. The former looks for glory from men, the latter finds its highest glory in God, the witness of a good conscience.[28]

Because human nature is intrinsically and holistically flawed, and because it will not be perfected until the end of time, the earthly city—whether it be Marxist, fascist, democratic, or otherwise—will never eradicate the Fall and so never bring Heaven to Earth. As Pascal said, "Man is neither angel nor beast, and it is unfortunately the case that anyone attempting to act as an angel ends up as a beast."[29] Many ersatz angels have led revolutions against human nature and Christian tradition. All have failed. Most have failed miserably and catastrophically, as the long shadow of Marxism reveals.

All utopian forms of government fail to understand the severity and pervasiveness of original sin, or they redefine it and then to try fix society through impossible means. Instead of seeing all human beings as partakers in original sin, CRT divides society into the oppressors and the oppressed based on race and gender. Instead of realizing that all hostilities among people cannot be legislated away, it isolates all inequalities as based on racism and sexism and advocates draconian measures to create "equity" through force of law and socialist government.[30]

Audacious as it might seem, this chapter argues that a Christian concept of God, the cosmos, humanity, and society provides the truest and richest account of our days on Earth—and of the afterlife. To apply a Christian understanding of CRT and its related issues is not reactionary, regressive, or arbitrary. On the contrary, the Christian worldview explains why the world exists as it does. It explains human beings as deposed royalty (both great and miserable) and how these dispossessed kings and queens can be reinstated before God through Jesus Christ. And it charts a wise approach to civil government, which emphasizes freedom of conscience, universal human rights, and the limits of earthly success for the city of man.

Any real racial reckoning or progress in racial relations is better served by a Christian worldview than by any version of CRT. Of course, Christians and others will interpret the history and social situation of POC in America differently than I have, although I have tried to make my case judiciously and with copious documentation. But however we may disagree on these matters, the Christian worldview—and the wisdom and power of the living God Himself—offers us the surest framework for both understanding our times and serving God, neighbor, and stranger in every sphere of life.

CHAPTER NINE

FANNING HOLY FLAMES

*"I am sending you out like sheep among wolves. There-
fore be as shrewd as snakes and as innocent as doves."*

—Jesus Christ (Matthew 10:16)

C ritical Race Theory and its related philosophies do not give us the
answers we need to face our challenges regarding race, gender,
economics, or anything else. They have, rather, sparked an inferno of
untruth, violence, hatred, fear, and unjust revolution. There is—and
will be more—deadly fire in the streets, because it is stoked and fueled
by the unholy fire in the minds of men and women. A man who
understood the power of ideas and the course of Western history,
Francis Schaeffer, put it well:

> People are unique in the inner life of the mind—what they
> are in their thought world determines how they act. This is
> true of their value systems and it is true of their creativity. It
> is true of their corporate actions, such as political decisions,
> and it is true of their personal lives. The results of their
> thought world flow through their fingers or from their

tongues into the external world. This is true of Michelangelo's chisel, and it is true of a dictator's sword.[1]

And it is true of a rioter's bomb, baton, and bullhorn. This book is an effort to put out the destructive fires of these untrue, anti-American, and dangerous ideologies with truth, facts, evidence, and sound reasoning. But how might we fan the flames of the American creed and serve God and neighbor in order to light fires that give warmth and light to our distressing condition? Let us succinctly consider several ways.

The Lordship of Christ

Before loyalty to one's country should come loyalty to our Creator and Redeemer God. The first command is to love God with all our being. The second is to love our neighbor as ourselves (Matthew 22:37–39). The God revealed propositionally in the Bible, as well as in nature and through history, is the holy Lord of all nations and peoples and is the Judge of all the earth. He is transcendent (above us) and immanent (with us); He is a personal being and not an impersonal force, principle, or substance (Isaiah 57:15). He holds us accountable and offers Himself to us in holy love, justice, and power. All people are called to know our Father in Heaven through the saving work of His Son, Jesus Christ, through the inspiration of the Holy Spirit. The triune God is worth knowing and serving. He is the highest court of appeal, the standard for truth, our only true good, and our source of strength. The masterful apologist C. S. Lewis brilliantly captures this in *Mere Christianity*:

God made us: invented us as a man invents an engine. A car is made to run on petrol, and it would not run properly on anything else. Now God designed the human machine to run on Himself. He Himself is the fuel our spirits were designed to burn, or the food our spirits were designed to feed on. There is no other. That is why it is just no good asking God to make us happy in our own way without bothering about religion. God cannot give us a happiness and peace apart from Himself, because it is not there.[2]

In our struggles to define America properly, to conserve what is good about it, to amend its errors, and to strengthen what is weak, we need to reckon Jesus Christ as Lord, the Master of all. The Apostles' Creed comes before the American creed.[3] Nations are not eternally secure, yet we wish, hope, pray, and work to the end that the American experiment may endure for many years more, that the American creed be restored and obeyed. Jesus Christ, however, is eternal and eternally trustworthy.

"Jesus Christ is the same yesterday and today and forever" (Hebrews 13:8). As such, He takes the place of supremacy in our efforts. Francis Schaeffer called this "the lordship of Christ over the whole of life." After His death and resurrection, Jesus affirmed that He had "all authority in heaven and on earth" and that on this sure basis, His followers should "disciple the nations" (Matthew 28:18–20). If He is Lord, then we should obey Him as He gives us strength through the Holy Spirit. As Schaeffer wrote in the context of art:

> When a man comes under the blood of Christ, his whole capacity as man is refashioned. His soul is saved, yes, but so are his mind and body. As Christians we are to look to Christ day by day, for Christ will produce his fruit through us. True spirituality means the lordship of Christ over the total man.[4]

The lordship of Christ applies to prayer, fellowship, worship, and Bible study, as well as to one's engagement in culture and in politics. As Dutch statesman, theologian, and Netherlands Prime Minister Abraham Kuyper (1837–1920), said, "There is not a square inch in the whole domain of our human existence over which Christ, who is Sovereign over all, does not cry, 'Mine.'"[5] Kuyper was not advocating a Christian theocracy, but for Christian involvement in all of life for the common good and for God's honor and glory. Schaeffer was doing the same when he wrote:

> True spirituality cannot be abstracted from truth at one end, nor from the whole man and the whole culture at the other. If there is a true spirituality, it must encompass all. The Bible insists that truth is one—and it is almost the sole surviving system in our generation that does.[6]

In light of the lordship of Christ and true spirituality, three imperatives will be commended. We need (1) truth in our minds, (2) fire in our bones, and (3) love in our hearts. In other words, our character must lead the way to social change for the better and not be sacrificed for popularity or expediency. In the words of the nineteenth century British statesman George Canning, "My road must be through character to power; I will try no other course; and I am sanguine enough to believe that this course, though not perhaps the quickest, is the surest."[7]

Truth in Our Minds

As noted, in an age of uncritical ideology and media distortions, wise people must seek the truth about issues pertaining to CRT. As Pascal wrote in approximately 1670, "Truth is so obscured nowadays and lies so well established that unless we love the truth, we shall never recognize it."[8] Those zealous for good causes can easily put results over truth and influence over knowledge. But any victories won outside of a strong allegiance to truth are hollow indeed, and may end up as defeats. Power politics and ideological thinking—whether from the right or left—often leaves truth behind in its pursuit of pure control. May it never be for us. If anyone can refute the claims made in this book, I invite them to try. Only the truth will set anyone free, as Jesus said (John 8:31).

As I have argued, the American system is essentially sound, although it is now fragile and imperiled by CRT and likeminded radicals. We can work within this system in order to bring reforms that conform to the American creed. Spin, propaganda, image-mongering, gaslighting,[9] and outright lies may be effective, but they must be anathema to us. So often when I hear politicians and activists speak, I wish I could quote this Scripture, which identifies those eternally doomed and excluded from the final City-Garden-Temple of God: "Outside are the dogs, those who practice magic arts, the sexually immoral, the murderers, the idolaters *and everyone who loves and practices falsehood*" (Revelation 22:15, emphasis added).

Fire in Our Bones

The paramount truths of life should not lie cold and inert within us, like unseen and unlit coals, but should rather burn as a holy fire to inspire us to shed light and bring the warmth of reality to the world. The hour is late. Hear the prophet Amos's words to the leaders of his nation:

> Woe to you who are complacent in Zion, and to you who feel secure on Mount Samaria, you notable men of the

foremost nation, to whom the people of Israel come!
(Amos 6:1)

And consider the Hebrew prophet Jeremiah, who was called to
the literally thankless task of proclaiming God's judgment against his
own rebellious nation. Often called, "the weeping prophet," Jeremiah
nonetheless had to stay true to the truth of God for his day. As he
cried out:

> Whenever I speak, I cry out
> proclaiming violence and destruction.
> So the word of the LORD has brought me
> insult and reproach all day long.
> But if I say, "I will not mention his word
> or speak anymore in his name,"
> his word is in my heart like a fire,
> a fire shut up in my bones.
> I am weary of holding it in;
> indeed, I cannot. (Jeremiah 20:8–9)

Will "violence and destruction" be the final chapter of the American experiment? Since I am neither a prophet nor the son of a prophet,
I cannot say. However, Os Guinness, who is a Christian statesman
nonpareil, our leading social critic, and a British connoisseur of the
American creed, is deeply worried. He believes that "the American
republic is as deeply divided today as at any time since just before the
Civil War."[10] He goes on in ways not surprising to those who have
read this book:

> The deepest division is between two mutually exclusive
> views of America: those who understand America and

freedom from the perspective of 1776 and the American Revolution, and those who understand America and freedom from the perspective of 1789 and the French Revolution and its ideological heirs. Such current movements as postmodernism, political correctness, tribal and identity politics, the sexual revolution, critical theory (or grievance studies), and socialism all come down from 1789 and have nothing to do with the ideas of 1776.[11]

Guinness, our Alexis de Tocqueville,[12] moved to our shores from England in the early 1980s in hopes that through his writing and speaking he might help "strengthen the things that remain" (Revelation 3:2) of American greatness and to warn it of its decline.[13] He has repeatedly instructed his adopted country of its potential and of the grave dangers of moving from the God-fearing and liberty-loving spirit of 1776 to that of the totalitarian, socialist, and secular spirit of the French Revolution of 1789, whose vision and values also animated the horrendous Marxist revolutions of 1917 led by Lenin in Russia and that of 1949 led by Mao Zedong in China. As I have argued, CRT advocates and their allies, given their Marxist roots, are the ideological heirs of 1789, 1917, and 1949 as well. This is why they must be resisted.

But the fire in the bones of Os Guinness never led him to be bellicose, acerbic, or outraged. Rather, he has been a genial and sagacious model for all those who love America, fear for her future, and fear God even more (Proverbs 1:7).

A biblical example of fire and grace is the Apostle Paul on mission. When he beheld the idolatry of the great classical city of Athens, he was more impressed by its idolatry than by its intellectual heritage.

While Paul was waiting for [Silas and Timothy] in Athens, he was greatly distressed to see that the city was full of idols. So he reasoned in the synagogue with both Jews and God-fearing Greeks, as well as in the marketplace day by day with those who happened to be there. (Acts 17:16–17)

The Greek word for "greatly distressed" is *emphatic*; Paul was no indifferent observer. The Message version, which is a paraphrase, captures the emotion well: "The longer Paul waited in Athens for Silas and Timothy, the angrier he got—all those idols! The city was a junkyard of idols." Lest America the beautiful become a "junkyard of idols," we need the kind of passion Paul possessed. It was a reasonable passion and a passionate reason, because it led him to try to persuade the Athenian philosophers of their errors (see Acts 17:17–34). Again, to Paul: "Follow my example, as I follow the example of Christ" (1 Corinthians 11:1).

Love in Our Hearts

We are to love our neighbors as ourselves (Matthew 22:38). But for at least thirty years, Americans have heard the language and fought the battles of a "culture war" over the American identity as it relates to the family, civil government, education, media, art, and entertainment. And it is hard to love others while at war with them. Sociologist James Davidson Hunter captured this in his landmark 1991 book, *Culture Wars: The Struggle to Define America*.[14] Those holding to traditional views on marriage, abortion, and sexual ethics were pitted against those who wanted to redefine America through progressive or liberal values that decenter the nuclear family, allow for abortion on demand, and favor sexual permissiveness. The battles are fought in the press, the schools, the courts, the arts, and at the ballot box. Now we face battles over CRT and its related issues, such as socialism, reparations, cultural appropriation, and more.

While warfare language is apt given the exigency of the issues and the far-reaching consequences of ideas, the metaphor of *war* can lead us astray. The Bible employs the argot of warfare concerning struggles in the spiritual world. We need to put on "the full armor" of God—helmet, breastplate, belt, footgear, shield, and sword (and with prayer)—to stand against the threatening evil powers at large (Ephesians 6:10–20). But these are metaphors, since Christians are not called to advance the Gospel through physical battles. Overly militaristic or triumphalist thinking and speaking should be avoided, especially the phrases "Take back America" or, worse yet, "Take back America for God." Those saying these things may simply mean that they want to restore what is good about the American creed and do so for the glory of God. However, these phrases will be heard by many as imperious cries for theocracy (which they are not).

Paul likewise makes this point when writing to the Corinthian church about disputes over his authority as an apostle.

> For though we live in the world, we do not wage war as the world does. The weapons we fight with are not the weapons of the world. On the contrary, they have divine power to demolish strongholds. We demolish arguments and every pretension that sets itself up against the knowledge of God, and we take captive every thought to make it obedient to Christ. (2 Corinthians 10:3–5)

These examples demonstrate that disputes need to be rightly engaged. Mere outrage is never enough, and rage is a work of the flesh, not of the Holy Spirit (Galatians 5:20). Spiritual battles require spiritual armor. Destroying strongholds of error—of whatever stripe— requires not worldly ways of warfare, but divinely authorized counterarguments. In other words, we need to do the Lord's work in the Lord's way—and that is the way of love.

Love does not shrink from controversy or minimize sin. Nor does it deny it has enemies. Loving your enemies does not mean pretending that they are your friends.[15] However, love obeys the golden rule of Jesus: "So in everything, do to others what you would have them do to you, for this sums up the Law and the Prophets" (Matthew 7:12). Some who may seem to be enemies can be disarmed and thoughtfully engaged through respect and love.

Thus, whether you are talking to a friend, challenging a professor, contacting an elected official, running for office, or speaking at a school board meeting, love should be the rule and truth should be the goal. Paul desired for the church to reach the point where it was no longer

> blown here and there by every wind of teaching and by the cunning and craftiness of people in their deceitful scheming. Instead, speaking the truth in love, we will grow to become in every respect the mature body of him who is the head, that is, Christ. From him the whole body, joined and held together by every supporting ligament, grows and builds itself up in love, as each part does its work. (Ephesians 4:14–16)

The operative phrase is "speaking the truth in love" (4:15). The Greek word for "speak" means more than talking; it means radiating or broadcasting love in all that we do, not just through verbalizing. Truth without love is harsh. Love without truth is mute and mushy. We need to live out the truth in love, in the church, in politics, and everywhere. One necessary step is to resist contempt for those with whom we disagree.[16] Contempt places others beneath us as unworthy of fair treatment. It takes discipline to strongly disagree with another's political views, but not hold them in contempt. We should try, with God helping us.

This love is rooted in God's love for us, shown through Jesus Christ's life, death, and resurrection; in our love for God; in our love for our neighbor; and in our love for our enemies. By this God-oriented and Spirit-sustained love, people will know that Christian advocacy and activism is not the commotion of another special interest group; it is not the machinations of a pressure group; it is not the agitations of malcontents hankering for a shouting (or shooting) match. It does not attack police stations, court houses, or political capitols. It does not confuse the cross with the flag. It does not yell insults at a school board meeting. It does not burn down anything. It does not threaten to burn down anything. It does not heckle, hassle, or tackle police officers. It does not hurl insulting epithets. Love may walk a dark and lonely road, but it is the right road. Jesus's challenge and promise are just as appropriate for social action and political change as they are for any other area of life.

> A new command I give you: Love one another. As I have
> loved you, so you must love one another. By this everyone
> will know that you are my disciples, if you love one another.
> (John 13:34–35)

If Christians truly love one another—even those with whom we disagree politically—and love those on the other side of every issue to which they are committed, then we will speak the truth in love for all to witness. The results of all our efforts are in God's hands. As Guinness says, "But whether the call is to be a loyal Remnant or to witness a Revival and a Reformation, there must be a rigorous practice of Truth and Love."[17]

Just in case "love" still seems slightly vague, I will again hand the microphone to the Apostle Paul.

> Love is patient, love is kind. It does not envy, it does not boast, it is not proud. It does not dishonor others, it is not self-seeking, it is not easily angered, it keeps no record of wrongs. Love does not delight in evil but rejoices with the truth. It always protects, always trusts, always hopes, always perseveres. Love never fails. (1 Corinthians 13:4–8)

CRT advocates have often failed to love in this way, however warm their hearts may sometimes be. Theirs is a vision of resentment, suspicion, unforgiveness, and even revenge. They take their grievances to the streets, and it often gets ugly, as witnessed in the firestorm summer of 2020. The great divide between the civil rights vision of Reverend Martin Luther King Jr. and his associates and that of CRT advocates is not only philosophical, but also practical. Dr. King did not accept a racist status quo; but neither did he endorse the ways of hate and violence evidenced by black nationalists such as Malcolm X and the Nation of Islam.[18] He and his followers would protest, but peacefully. They would break unjust laws, but not by destroying anything. If arrested, they would go to jail, taking up their crosses. When released, they would return to their nonviolent protests until things were set right.

Dr. King wrote a book called *Strength to Love*[19] and a brilliant essay on natural law and civil resistance from a jail cell in August of 1963, "Letter from Birmingham Jail."[20] Love sent him to jail, not hatred of any white person and certainly not hatred for America, since he believed that his people could finally fully benefit from America's founding ideals found in the Declaration of Independence. Simply read and/or listen to his "I Have a Dream" (1963) speech to verify this.[21]

As my wife and I watched Shelby Steele's documentary, *What Killed Michael Brown?* (2020), we were moved by its juxtaposition of footage from the peaceful and effective civil rights demonstrations in the 1950s and '60s over against the violent and hate-filled riots of the summer of 2020. Old black-and-white footage showed black people dressed in suits being hammered by white police and brutally knocked over by water shot from fire hoses. Color footage from the summer of 2020 showed rioters screaming epithets, hurling objects, burning buildings, and calling for the end of the American experiment.

John Lewis (1940–2020) was a young follower of Martin Luther King Jr. in the Civil Rights Movement. He absorbed his peaceful but insistent methods of social protest through civil disobedience. Mr. Lewis served in the House of Representatives for Georgia's fifth congressional district from 1987 until his death in 2020. He was often arrested, beaten, and accosted for his activism. He called this "getting into good trouble."[22] He and I would disagree on many matters, but he retained the spirit of the Civil Rights Movement until the end, pleading with violent protesters in 2020 to stop rioting, but to keep protesting.[23] He prepared a book shortly before his death, which was published posthumously and which defined his basic ideas. In *Carry On: Reflections for a New Generation*, he wrote.

> Destruction doesn't work. Rioting isn't a movement. We must be constructive and not destructive. Chaos is sowing more division and discord.... When you burn down a building or topple a car, the violence drowns out the injustice that's being done to you. It puts you on the same moral level as the people whose violence you are protesting. You're no longer on the higher ground or plane. You make enemies of the people you need to win over to effect change.[24]

Heart Matters

Although I disagree with CRT's interrogation of all white people as racist in one way or another—since I challenge the claim that America is "systemically racist"—white folks (and all folks) should search their hearts before God and in prayer to see if they harbor any racial antagonisms. It is easy to fail in this area, given all the rancor, ridicule, and riots. As King David wrote,

> Search me, God, and know my heart;
> test me and know my anxious thoughts.
> See if there is any offensive way in me,
> and lead me in the way everlasting. (Psalm 139:23–24)

We can also ask the God who shows no favoritism to protect us from any racial stereotypes or resentment. "Above all else, guard your heart, for everything you do flows from it" (Proverbs 4:23).

Since we can be blind to our own faults—racial or otherwise—we need help from others; in this case, if we are white, we should have conversations with POC on the matters this book addresses. If we are a POC, then we should have discussions with those who are not. Of course, some will agree with us; others will not.[25] But we should push beyond questions of policy—as important as these are—to personal character. How loving have we been to those who look different than we do or who differ from us on CRT? How might we need to reform our attitudes and actions?

Prayer for Our Country

I have mentioned prayer several times in this book, but let us briefly consider prayer for America in light of our present crises. Prayer takes many forms—such as praise, contrition, petition, lament, and intersession—but the Bible exhorts us to pray for our political leaders. The Apostle Paul wrote this to Timothy (and to us):

> I urge, then, first of all, that petitions, prayers, intercession and thanksgiving be made for all people—for kings and all those in authority, that we may live peaceful and quiet lives in all godliness and holiness. This is good, and pleases God our Savior. (1 Timothy 2:1–3)

Since "righteousness exalts a nation, but sin condemns any people" (Proverbs 14:34), we should beseech the Lord to bring repentance to our leaders and to all citizens, and to give us all wisdom and courage to renew our Republic under God and for the common good. Since, as the Psalmist writes, "Can a corrupt throne be allied with you—a throne that brings on misery by its decrees?" (Psalm 94:20), we should beseech the Lord to expose evil and corruption in civil government and to replace it with better people who can live truer to our best American ideas and ideals. Since Christians represent Christ on earth and are salt and light, we should beseech the Lord to purify and strengthen the church in America, come what may (Matthew 5:1-16).

As Os Guinness has repeatedly warned, America faces its greatest crisis of identity since the Civil War.

> For admirers of America today, sleep has become fitful. The great American republic is in the throes of its gravest crisis since the Civil War, a crisis that threatens its greatness, its freedom, and its character.[26]

As such, we need a spirit of national repentance and prayer. I cannot think of a better model than the following Resolution 97, issued by Abraham Lincoln on March 30, 1863, which deserves to be quoted in full:

> Proclamation 97—Appointing a Day of National Humiliation, Fasting, and Prayer
>
> March 30, 1863
>
> Whereas the Senate of the United States, devoutly recognizing the supreme authority and just government of Almighty God in all the affairs of men and of nations, has by a resolution requested the President to designate and set apart a day for national prayer and humiliation; and
>
> Whereas it is the duty of nations as well as of men to own their dependence upon the overruling power of God, to confess their sins and transgressions in humble sorrow, yet with assured hope that genuine repentance will lead to mercy and pardon, and to recognize the sublime truth, announced in the Holy Scriptures and proven by all history, that those nations only are blessed whose God is the Lord;
>
> And, insomuch as we know that by His divine law nations, like individuals, are subjected to punishments and chastisements in this world, may we not justly fear that the awful calamity of civil war which now desolates the land may be but a punishment inflicted upon us for our presumptuous sins, to the needful end of our national reformation as a whole people? We have been the recipients of the choicest bounties of Heaven; we have been preserved these many years in peace and prosperity; we have grown in numbers, wealth, and power as no other nation has ever grown. But

we have forgotten God. We have forgotten the gracious hand which preserved us in peace and multiplied and enriched and strengthened us, and we have vainly imagined, in the deceitfulness of our hearts, that all these blessings were produced by some superior wisdom and virtue of our own. Intoxicated with unbroken success, we have become too self-sufficient to feel the necessity of redeeming and preserving grace, too proud to pray to the God that made us.

It behooves us, then, to humble ourselves before the offended Power, to confess our national sins, and to pray for clemency and forgiveness.

Now, therefore, in compliance with the request, and fully concurring in the views of the Senate, I do by this my proclamation designate and set apart Thursday, the 30th day of April, 1863, as a day of national humiliation, fasting, and prayer. And I do hereby request all the people to abstain on that day from their ordinary secular pursuits, and to unite at their several places of public worship and their respective homes in keeping the day holy to the Lord and devoted to the humble discharge of the religious duties proper to that solemn occasion.

All this being done in sincerity and truth, let us then rest humbly in the hope authorized by the divine teachings that the united cry of the nation will be heard on high and answered with blessings no less than the pardon of our national sins and the restoration of our now divided and suffering country to its former happy condition of unity and peace. In witness whereof I have hereunto set my hand and caused the seal of the United States to be affixed.

Done at the city of Washington, this 30th day of March,
A. D. 1863, and of the Independence of the United States
the eighty-seventh.
ABRAHAM LINCOLN.
By the President:
WILLIAM H. SEWARD, *Secretary of State*.[27]

Oh, for a new Abraham Lincoln to help lead us today!

Education: Back to First Things

Having outlined a model of getting truth in our minds, fire in our
bones, and love in our hearts, and having exhorted us to pray, we
move to specific social action, starting with education.

Much of what I take for granted is unknown by many younger
than myself, especially millennials and Generation Z. I resist the easy
stereotypes of "generationalism" (which Os Guinness calls "a secular
form of astrology"), since people need to be treated as individuals,
but many surveys and my general observations indicate that younger
people are ignorant of both the American creed and the failures and
outright evils of socialism, and they gravitate toward "social justice"
causes in alignment with CRT. This is wrong, and only education
counters perilous ignorance.

Just as the Christian faith is theoretically only one generation
away from extinction, so the American creed must be passed down
faithfully if it is to be lived out over time. The general principle is laid
down in the Pentateuch and spoken by God Himself to His people:

Hear, O Israel: The LORD our God, the LORD is one. Love
the LORD your God with all your heart and with all your
soul and with all your strength. These commandments that

I give you today are to be on your hearts. Impress them on your children. Talk about them when you sit at home and when you walk along the road, when you lie down and when you get up. Tie them as symbols on your hands and bind them on your foreheads. Write them on the door-frames of your houses and on your gates. (Deuteronomy 6:4–9)

As the late public theologian Richard John Neuhaus often said, "America is an experiment in ordered liberty."[28] Experiments can fail over time, and the *American* experiment is unique and fragile enough that it requires great care to be preserved intact. Thomas Jefferson is often wrongly cited as saying, "An educated citizenry is a vital requisite for our survival as a free people."[29] While this is true, we must press well beyond it. We need the right kind of education, and we should strive for more than the mere survival of a free people. A republic such as ours—exceptional among the nations—necessitates republican virtue in order to be sustained. At a minimum, we need to know our true history, as President Ronald Reagan noted in his farewell address on January 11, 1989:

> Younger parents aren't sure that an unambivalent appreciation of America is the right thing to teach modern children. And as for those who create the popular culture, well-grounded patriotism is no longer the style.... We've got to do a better job of getting across that America is freedom—freedom of speech, freedom of religion, freedom of enterprise. And freedom is special and rare. It's fragile; it needs protection.
>
> So, we've got to teach history based not on what's in fashion but what's important.... I'm warning of an

eradication of the American memory that could result, ultimately, in an erosion of the American spirit. Let's start with some basics: more attention to American history and a greater emphasis on civic ritual.[30]

I will return to the idea of "civic ritual" below. Every citizen needs to understand what America is about and what it means to be an American citizen. Victor Davis Hanson has written of "the dying citizen" in America given the flood of illegal immigration, progressivism, globalism, tribalism (identity politics), and more.[31] Nevertheless, citizenship can be taught in the home, at the school, and in the church. In his bracing and alarming book, *A Free People's Suicide*, Os Guinness writes of "the golden triangle" needed to support the American experiment and the American creed. *Liberty* requires *virtue*, which requires *faith*. Liberty is not license; it is the freedom to follow virtue (what is morally good); and Christian faith is the best—but not the only—support for virtue. Those outside of Christianity, such as conservative Jews, advance a moral vision with which Christians can agree.[32]

The meaning of American citizenship is well expressed by my colleague, Dr. Sung Wook Chung, a native of South Korea and a professor of theology at Denver Seminary. When I asked him to write of why he became a United States citizen, he wrote this:

> I have become an American citizen primarily because of religious freedom. I want to enjoy liberty to worship the triune God and to practice my faith as freely as possible without any external hindrance and interference. America is, more than anything else, a symbol of religious freedom.
>
> Secondly, I have become an American citizen because of its promotion of human dignity and rights. Of course, I

am aware that America still has serious problems in relation to human rights issues, especially racial conflict. Nevertheless, America is far more advanced in promoting human rights and dignity than any other country in the world, including South Korea, my home country.

Thirdly, I have become an American citizen because of the fact that America does remain an open society. Despite many problems of media's distortions and misinformation, I can enjoy freedom of expression and ideas in America more than any other country in the whole globe.[33]

Those who become naturalized citizens from other countries often learn more about America than many native-born Americans. This ought not be. We should teach about America's heritage—the good, the bad, and the ugly—in homeschooling, private education, public education, and in the church. That includes our history of race relations. However, as I have argued, we should not teach that America is based on slavery (the 1619 boogey), that it is systemically racist (CRT doctrine), or that it is irredeemable on race (Derrick Bell). Our national motto is *E Pluribis Unum*—out of the many, one; and this is written on the Great Seal of America. But what is the "one," the unity amidst the diversity? A strong civic education can answer that vital question and give a backbone to what we have in common as Americans. A quick test on anyone's knowledge of the American creed is to ask someone (or yourself): "What are the five freedoms of the First Amendment"? Everyone can ask himself or herself to affirm what all nationalized citizens must affirm.

I hereby declare, on oath, that I absolutely and entirely renounce and abjure all allegiance and fidelity to any foreign prince, potentate, state, or sovereignty, of whom or

which I have heretofore been a subject or citizen; that I will
support and defend the Constitution and laws of the United
States of America against all enemies, foreign and domestic;
that I will bear true faith and allegiance to the same; that
I will bear arms on behalf of the United States when
required by the law; that I will perform noncombatant
service in the Armed Forces of the United States when
required by the law; that I will perform work of national
importance under civilian direction when required by the
law; and that I take this obligation freely, without any
mental reservation or purpose of evasion; so help me God.[34]

State Schools and the Alternatives

Compulsory education did not arrive in America with the
Mayflower. It was instituted much later, and with motives not entirely
savory. Rather than address this vexed matter,[35] consider the state of
state education today. It is said that "politics is downstream from
culture," and culture is shaped by education, as is education shaped
by culture. The culture of Hollywood films is not far from what is
taught about moral values in state education. The fictions of the 1619
Project are taught in more than four thousand K–12 state schools, and
its principal author, Nikole Hannah-Jones, won a Pulitzer Prize.
When Hannah-Jones was interviewed on *Meet the Press* about the
1619 curriculum being used in public schools, she said,

I don't really understand this idea that parents should
decide what's being taught. I'm not a professional educator.
I don't have a degree in social studies or science. We send
our children to school because we want them to be taught
by people who have an expertise in the subject area.[36]

Certainly, educators should be educated in how to educate, but the idea that parents—who are taxed for public schools and who send their own flesh-and-blood to these schools—should not decide (or at least have a strong say) what is taught, is elitist and statist to the core. It should be resisted. The sexual morality of the LGBTQ world is advocated in state schools as well, as are anti-American, anti-Christian, and pro-socialist ideas. This is not uniform, but it is sadly common and corrodes the national character at the earliest ages. We can hope that students will pay attention in math and drift off when moral values are taught, but that is unrealistic.

Given the realities of state education—which can never teach a Christian worldview, among its other limitations[37]—parents and grandparents should seriously consider putting their children in a traditional private school, a microschool,[38] or practice home-schooling.[39] If that is not financially possible, many charter schools are a healthier alternative, because they involve parents more directly, are freer from the leftist teachers' unions than other state schools, and have a proven record of success, especially with disadvantaged children, many of whom are POC. Thomas Sowell establishes this point in *Charter Schools and Their Enemies*.[40] Some charter schools affirm historic American values, are friendly to the Judeo-Christian tradition, emphasize citizenship, and eschew CRT indoctrination.[41] Of course, these will come under increasing fire if the CRT ideology continues to infiltrate all aspects of culture.[42] A web page monitors the intrusion of CRT in public schools and will be helpful for parents and grandparents.[43]

Another way to challenge the CRT agenda is to advocate for school choice in public education. When parents decide which school is best for their children, they can choose schools closer to their worldview and political beliefs. It also requires that state schools compete with other schools, which encourages improvement. This is accomplished through the voucher system (or scholarship programs) and is especially helpful for lower-income families, many of whom are POC. Some claim school choice began with racist motivations as a way to fight desegregation, but that is exactly the opposite of the truth.[44] "As early as 1955, economists such as [Milton] Friedman began touting vouchers as a strategy to expedite integration."[45]

Beyond K–12 education, we should remember that state universities are profoundly leftist, secular, and pro-CRT in their curricula and pedagogy. This is not uniform, but it is the norm. I know. All my degrees are from state universities, and I was a campus minister for twelve years. Conservative speakers are routinely deplatformed or are even placed in physical danger if they appear at a state university or secular college. If one attends this kind of institution, he or she needs to be well-prepared for the onslaught, especially in the humanities. Churches should help by teaching college preparation classes—as I have done—for their high school students that explain and defend the biblical worldview[46] and advance the Judeo-Christian contributions to the American creed.

While at college, students should stay in close fellowship with other Christians. At a minimum, they should be involved in a Bible-believing church and perhaps in a campus ministry if their church does not have one. Although I have not focused on this, many Christian organizations and churches support CRT, either explicitly or implicitly. If what I have written here is correct, they have gone astray. So one must be discerning. Other books have ably addressed the Christian embrace of CRT, such as *Fault Lines* by Voddie Baucham[47] and *Christianity and Wokeness* by Owen Strachan.[48] Students may want to seek out conservative political groups on campus for teaching and encouragement. If none are on campus, national student organizations, such as the Young America's

Foundation (yaf.org) and PragerForce (prageru.com/pragerforce) can be consulted for help.

Civic Rituals

Humans live by rituals of all kinds.[49] They may be individual (daily Bible reading), familial (prayer before dinner together), church (the sermon, the Lord's supper, etc.), or civic. Nations need civil rituals, as President Reagan said in his farewell speech. Rituals remind us of our identity and what we should value. The following are a few civic rituals to observe yearly.

The Fourth of July celebrates our independence from England, although that is often lost amidst the fireworks and cookouts. It is better called Independence Day so that we remember the birth of the United States. Families might read aloud all or part of the Declaration on July Fourth, pray for America, and watch a patriotic film or play. America is a nation like no other, and its origin should be remembered and celebrated. Moreover, we should strive to live up to its founding ideals, which is an ongoing struggle for all Americans. Os Guinness has a good idea.

> Might it be that instead of celebrating the Fourth of July with a military-style parade to celebrate the strength of the armed forces, Americans could commemorate the Fourth with a Hebrew-style national rededication on the National Mall, acknowledging the sins and failures of the past and present, reaffirming the first principles of the American experiment, and recommitting themselves to the uniting first principles of the American Unum to balance the American Pluribus?[50]

Although celebrated less often, *Constitution Week* is worth celebrating since our Constitution is a self-reforming marvel of liberty and the rule of law, as I have argued.[51] This is a fine time to read through the Constitution, and/or a good book on the Constitution, take a class on the Constitution,[52] or to attend events commemorating it. "U.S. Constitution Week," which began in 2011, is held in Grand Lake, Colorado, and features speakers, music, contests, and more.[53]

The observance of *Veterans Day* focuses us on those who served America in the armed forces. America is worth defending, so remembering and honoring veterans is an appropriately patriotic act. Whenever I find that someone I know is serving or has served in the military, I thank them for it. Many who have served in wars have paid a high price through PTSD, physical injury, marriage breakdown, and more. They should be thanked and helped.

The often-neglected role played by black people in World War II should be remembered as well. Although they were often discriminated against and not allowed in combat roles, 1.2 million served. The "Tuskegee Airmen, the all-Black fighter pilot group trained at Tuskegee Institute in Alabama, escorted bombers over Italy and Sicily, flying 1,600 combat missions and destroying 237 German aircraft on ground and 37 in air."[54]

In 2021, President Joe Biden declared *Juneteenth* a national holiday. June 19 commemorates the end of slavery by marking the day enslaved people in Texas learned they were free. It was the first new federal holiday since Martin Luther King Jr. Day (January 17) was instituted in 1983 during the Reagan presidency.[55] Both Juneteenth and Martin Luther King Jr. Day mark out consequential factors in America's long and continuing effort to reach racial justice. Inasmuch as Dr. King and his racial philosophy are commemorated, CRT's deviation from it becomes clear. Black History Month (formerly a week) honors black achievement in all areas of life, not only concerning racial justice.[56] It, too, should be affirmed. As a jazz aficionado, I cannot imagine that art form without the contributions of African Americans.

Besides these annual observances, periodic rituals contribute to the recognition of the American Creed and the value of the American experiment. These include the singing of the national anthem and saying the Pledge of Allegiance. The national anthem has become controversial in recent years because of those who "take a knee" to show their solidarity with some vague sense of racial justice, often associated with Black Lives Matter. But the national anthem is not an endorsement of everything America has done, nor does it mean that America cannot improve. As such, there is no reason to draw attention to yourself by refusing to stand and place your hand over your heart. Nor is there any reason to associate with BLM, given what I and others have written.[57]

What of the Pledge of Allegiance? I said the pledge many times in public school in the 1960s in Anchorage, Alaska. However, many years later, I was pleasantly surprised when asked to recite it at an event held at Colorado Christian University. It is the school's tradition to recite the Pledge at major university events.

The Pledge of Allegiance was first published in *The Youth's Companion* on September 8, 1892. The wording has been changed several times, but this version was adopted in 1954:

> I pledge allegiance to the flag of the United States of America and to the Republic for which it stands, one Nation under God, indivisible, with liberty and justice for all.

"Under God" was added to the Pledge by Congress in 1954 at the height of the Cold War with the atheist regime, the USSR. The Pledge of Allegiance "should be rendered by standing at attention facing the flag with the right hand over the heart."

When not in uniform men should remove any non-religious headdress with their right hand and hold it at the left shoulder, the hand being over the heart. Persons in uniform should remain silent, face the flag, and render the military salute. Members of the Armed Forces not in uniform and veterans may render the military salute in the manner provided for persons in uniform.[58]

So instructs the *U.S. Code*, an official federal document seldom consulted. Not a few protests and riots in the United States in the summer of 2020 featured flag burnings, a sign of desecration of the symbol of America. Few things could be more un-American, anti-American, and alien to "life, liberty, and the pursuit of happiness" than flag burning. As Robert Bork notes succinctly, "burning a flag is not speech and should not fall under First Amendment protection."[59] Nevertheless, since the *Texas v. Johnson* Supreme Court case (1989), American flag burning is considered a constitutional right.

The Pledge is not a prayer, but it has a theological aspect, since it speaks of America as being "under God." That is no carte blanche endorsement of everything American. "Under God," on any Judeo-Christian reading, means under God's sovereign and holy audit, either in blessing or in judgment. God is no respecter of persons (Romans 2:11) and neither is He a respecter of nations in the sense of showing favoritism by adjusting moral standards from one nation to another (Joel 3; Isaiah 66; Revelation 13).

Fight Bad Fire with Good Fire

This book has advocated that we fight fire with fire. However, the fire I commend is not the fire that animates CRT and its allied advocates and activists. It does not spark violent protests, riots, hate fests, cancellations, or the dismantling of the American system by limiting free speech, vilifying all white people, or imposing socialism. This fire is a well-reasoned, knowledgeable, and humble conviction that the American creed is worth reaffirming and living by, that all people are created equal by a just and loving God, and that a virtuous citizenry is necessary for the moral and spiritual recovery from the perils we now face. What we all need is wisdom from above and moral courage. I will let the living and active Word of God (Hebrews 4:12) have the last word in this book, and it is my prayer for myself and my country.

> Who is wise and understanding among you? Let them show it by their good life, by deeds done in the humility that comes from wisdom. But if you harbor bitter envy and selfish ambition in your hearts, do not boast about it or deny the truth. Such "wisdom" does not come down from heaven but is earthly, unspiritual, demonic. For where you have envy and selfish ambition, there you find disorder and every evil practice.
>
> But the wisdom that comes from heaven is first of all pure; then peace-loving, considerate, submissive, full of mercy and good fruit, impartial and sincere. Peacemakers who sow in peace reap a harvest of righteousness. (James 3:13–18)

NOTES

Preface

1. The definitive critique of leftism is by Erik von Kuehnelt-Leddihn, *Leftism: from de Sade and Marx to Hitler and Marcuse* (New Rochelle, NY: Arlington House, 1974).
2. See Thomas Sowell's magisterial work, *A Conflict of Visions: Ideological Origins of Political Struggles* (New York: Basic Books, 2007).
3. David Horowitz, *Radicals: Portraits of a Destructive Passion* (Washington, D.C.: Regnery Publishing, 2012), 71.
4. Mark Moore, "BLM Leader, 'If Change Doesn't Happen, Then We'll Burn Down This System,'" *New York Post*, June 25, 2020, https://nypost.com /2020/06/25/blm-leader-if-change-doesnt-happen-we-will-burn-down-th is-system/.
5. The inspiration for the metaphor of fire comes from James H. Billington, *Fire in the Minds of Men: Origins of the Revolutionary Faith*, rev. ed. (Oxfordshire, EN: Routledge, 1998).

Introduction

1. I assess the facts of the matter in Section IV: "A Better Fire."
2. "U.S. Civil Unrest," Center for Disaster Philanthropy, June 25, 2021, https://disasterphilanthropy.org/disasters/u-s-civil-unrest/.
3. Jemima McEvoy, "14 Days of Protests, 19 Dead," *Forbes*, June 8, 2020, https://www.forbes.com/sites/jemimamcevoy/2020/06/08/14-days-of-pro tests-19-dead/?sh=3e43b5e94de4.
4. Douglas A. McIntyre, "Guns in America: Nearly 40 Million Guns Were Purchased Legally in 2020 and Another 4.1 Million Bought in January," *USA Today*, February 10, 2021, https://www.usatoday.com/story/money /2021/02/10/this-is-how-many-guns-were-sold-in-all-50-states/43371461/.
5. For a detailed assessment of these kinds of cases, see David Horowitz, *I Can't Breathe* (2021).
6. Vicky Osterweil, *In Defense of Looting* (New York: Bold Type Books, 2020). Perhaps stores might have difficulty keeping the book in stock if potential buyers heed the lesson and loot it. This was a problem with

another anarchist book, *Steal This Book* (1971) by Abbie Hoffman (1936–89).

7. Natalie Escobar, "One Author's Controversial View: 'In Defense of Looting,'" *Code Switch* (podcast), August 27, 2020, https://www.npr.org /sections/codeswitch/2020/08/27/906642178/one-authors-argument-in-de fense-of-looting.

8. Ibid.

9. Christopher F. Rufo, "Critical Race Theory: What It Is and How to Fight It," *Imprimis* 50, no. 3, (March 2021), https://imprimis.hillsdale.edu/criti cal-race-theory-fight/.

10. There is a separate discipline called Queer Studies that I will not directly address.

11. Merriam-Webster, "White Supremacy," https://www.merriam-webster .com/dictionary/white%20supremacy. See also: John Phillip Jenkins, "White Supremacy," Britannica online, https://www.britannica.com/top ic/white-supremacy.

12. See Douglas Groothuis, "Postmodernism on Race and Gender" in *Truth Decay* (Downers Grove, IL: InterVarsity Press, 2000).

13. Kimberlé Crenshaw, "Demarginalizing the Intersection of Race and Sex: A Black Feminist Critique of Antidiscrimination Doctrine, Feminist Theory, and Antiracist Policies," *University of Chicago Legal Forum* 1, no. 8 (1989): 139–167, https://chicagounbound.uchicago.edu/cgi/viewcont ent.cgi?article=1052&context=uclf.

14. See Alan Dershowitz, *The Case Against the New Censorship* (New York: Hot Books, 2021).

Chapter One: Fire in the Mind of Karl Marx and His Followers

1. A classic and bestselling critique is by Dr. Fred Shwarz (1913–2009), *You Can Trust the Communists (to be Communists)* (New York: Prentice-Hall, 1960).

2. I take this from Lloyd Billingsley's critique of the evangelical left called *The Generation that Knew Not Joseph: A Critique of Marxism and the Religious Left* (Portland, OR: Multnomah Press, 1985). Many "progressive" Christians today are making the same political mistakes made by the leftist Christians that Billingsley critiqued.

3. For an overview of these countries, with no political analysis, see Matt Rosenberg, "A List of Current Communist Countries in the World,"

ThoughtCo, April 11, 2020, https://www.thoughtco.com/communist-cou
ntries-overview-1435178.

4. Mike Sabo, "Educating Students about the Victims of Communism,"
    RealClearEducation, October 15, 2021, https://www.realcleareducation
    .com/articles/2021/10/15/educating_students_about_the_victims_of_com
    munism_110650.html.

5. Yaron Steinbuch, "Black Lives Matter Co-founder Describes Herself as
    'Trained Marxist,'" *New York Post*, June 25, 2020, https://nypost.com/20
    20/06/25/blm-co-founder-describes-herself-as-trained-marxist/.

6. Mike Gonzalez, *BLM: The Making of a New Marxist Revolution* (New
    York: Encounter, 2021).

7. Julia Carrie Wong, "The Bay Area Roots of Black Lives Matter," *SF
    Weekly,* November 11, 2015, https://www.sfweekly.com/news/the-bay-ar
    ea-roots-of-black-lives-matter/.

8. Fydor Dostoevsky, *Demons* (New York: Vintage Books, 1994), 94.

9. Stéphane Courtois et al., *The Black Book of Communism* (Cambridge,
    MA: Harvard University Press, 1999).

10. Christopher Brooks, "Historically Speaking: Critical Race Theory and Karl
    Marx's Racism," *Morning Call*, August 20, 2021, https://www.mcall.com
    /opinion/mc-opi-historically-speaking19-critical-race-theory-brooks-2021
    0820-6b6rhqtg25ctxichvuh3wmpkiq-story.html; Nathaniel Weyl, *Karl
    Marx, Racist* (Arlington House, 1979).

11. See Paul Kengor, *The Devil and Karl Marx* (Gastonia, NC: Tan Books,
    2020).

12. Paul Kengor, "Tearing Down with Marx," *Epoch Times*, September 9,
    2020, https://www.theepochtimes.com/tearing-down-with-marx_34921
    66.html. See also Richard Wurmbrand, *Marx and Satan* (Wheaton, IL:
    Crossway Books, 1986).

13. Karl Marx, *Theses on Feuerbach* (1845), Marxists.org, https://www.mar
    xists.org/archive/marx/works/1845/theses/theses.htm.

14. Karl Marx, *A Contribution to the Critique of Hegel's Philosophy of Right*
    (1842), Marxists.org, https://www.marxists.org/archive/marx/works/18
    43/critique-hpr/intro.htm.

15. For a thorough apologetic response to this claim, see Hans Kung, "A
    Consolation Serving Human Interests? Karl Marx," in *Does God Exist?*
    (New York: Simon and Schuster, 1980). We will also treat atheism in
    Chapter Eight: "A Christian Framework."

16. Marx, *A Contribution to the Critique of Hegel's Philosophy of Right*.

17. Ibid.
18. Karl Marx, *The Communist Manifesto* (Lawrence, KS: Neeland Media, [1848] 2017), 20, Kindle.
19. Atheism naturally leads to nihilism. See James Sire, "Zero Hour: Nihilism," in *The Universe Next Door: A Basic Worldview Catalogue*, 6th ed. (Downers Grove, IL: InterVarsity Press, 2020).
20. Mark Levin, *American Marxism* (New York: Threshold Editions, 2021), 4. And in more detail, see Thomas Sowell, "Marxian Value" in *Marxism: Philosophy and Economics* (New York: William Morrow, 1985).
21. Marx, *The Communist Manifesto*, 1.
22. Karl Marx, "Human Requirements and Division of Labour Under the Rule of Private Property," *Economic and Philosophical Manuscripts of 1844*, Marxists.org, https://www.marxists.org/archive/marx/works/1844/manu scripts/needs.htm.
23. Thomas Sowell, *Discrimination and Disparities* (New York: Basic Books, 2018), 27.
24. Marx, *The Communist Manifesto*, 17.
25. Engels is credited with the phrase "withering away," but he agreed with Marx on this. See Frederick Engels, *Socialism: Utopian and Scientific* (1880), Marxists.org, https://www.marxists.org/archive/marx/works/18 80/soc-utop/index.htm. Lenin further developed the idea in "The Withering Away of the State and Violent Revolution," *The State and Revolution* (1917), Marxists.org, https://www.marxists.org/archive/lenin/works/1917 /staterev/ch01.htm.
26. Karl Marx and Frederick Engels, *The German Ideology* (1845), Marxists. org, https://www.marxists.org/archive/marx/works/1845/german-ideolo gy/ch01a.htm#a4.
27. R. J. Rummel, "How Many Did Communist Regimes Murder?," 1993, https://www.hawaii.edu/powerkills/COM.ART.HTM. For the fuller story, see Rummel, *Death by Government* (New York: Routledge, 1997).
28. He is cited as calling for "a long march through the institutions," but the phrase is from German socialist activist Rudi Dutschke (1940–1979).
29. Felicity Barringer, "The Mainstreaming of Marxism on American Campuses," *New York Times*, October 25, 1989, https://www.nytimes .com/1989/10/25/us/education-the-mainstreaming-of-marxism-in-us-coll eges.html.
30. Stephen Eric Bronner, *Critical Theory: A Very Short Introduction* (Oxford: Oxford University Press, 2011), 9.

31. Ibid., 10–18. Other thinkers, such as Jürgen Habermas and John Lukas, contributed to this school of thought.
32. Ibid., 20.
33. Ibid., 24.
34. See Anne Applebaum, "How Stalin Hid Ukraine's Famine from the World," *Atlantic*, October 17, 2017, https://www.theatlantic.com/international/archive/2017/10/red-famine-anne-applebaum-ukraine-soviet-union/542610/. See her book *Red Famine, Stalin's War on Ukraine*.
35. Gonzalez, *BLM*, xxv, 48, 51, 66–67, 75–78, 154.
36. Ibid., 51, 83, 88–89. Davis wrote the forward to Patrisse Khan-Cullors and Asha Bandele's book *When They Call You a Terrorist: A Black Lives Matter Memoir* (New York: St. Martin's Griffin, 2020).
37. Bryan Magee gives an accurate description of Marcuse and the Frankfurt school in his introduction to this 1977 video of 43 minutes: Manufacturing Intellect, "Herbert Marcuse interview with Bryan Magee (1977)," YouTube, September 17, 2017, https://www.youtube.com/watch?v=0KqC1lTAJx4.
38. Herbert Marcuse, *One-Dimensional Man: Studies in the Ideology of Advanced Industrial Society* (Boston: Beacon Press, 1991).
39. Herbert Marcuse, *Eros and Civilization: A Philosophical Inquiry into Freud* (New York: Vintage Books, 1962), 184. *Cathexis* is a term from psychoanalysis that means an unhealthy concentration of mental energy on some object.
40. See Phillip Jennings, *The Politically Incorrect Guide to the Vietnam War* (Washington, D.C.: Regnery, 2010). See also Thomas Sowell, *Intellectuals and Society*, revised and enlarged ed. (New York: Basic Books, 2011), 341–48.
41. See Os Guinness, *The Dust of Death* (Westmont, IL: InterVarsity Press), 116.
42. See Thomas Sowell, *Marxism: Philosophy and Economics* (New York: William Morrow, 1985), 202–4.
43. Interview: "Herbert Marcuse, The Question of Revolution," *New Left Review* 1, no. 45 (September/October 1967), https://newleftreview.org/issues/i45/articles/herbert-marcuse-the-question-of-revolution.
44. Marcuse, *One-Dimensional Man*, 256–57.
45. Paul Kengor, "Commies Just Love Blacks and Women," in *The Politically Incorrect Guide to Communism* (Washington, D.C.: Regnery, 2017).

46. This is a 1990 video of Obama introducing Bell. PBS, Frontline, March 7, 2012, https://www.pbs.org/wgbh/frontline/article/the-story-behind-the-ob ama-law-school-speech-video/.

47. Quoted in Mark Levin, *American Marxism* (New York: Threshold Editions, 2021), 96.

48. See Daniel A. Farber and Suzanna Sherry, *Beyond All Reason: The Radical Assault on Truth in American Law* (New York: Oxford University Press, 1997), 87–88, 133–37, which speaks of a "paranoid style" that fits Bell.

Chapter Two: Fire in Our Own House

1. These words were inflammatory, but the context claimed that inasmuch as America mistreats blacks, then "God damn America." Still, it was essentially anti-American, and is hardly a message most Americans could support. Thus, Obama disassociated himself from Wright. See Brian Ross and Rehab El-Buri, "Obama's Pastor: God Damn America, U.S. to Blame for 9/11," ABC News, May 11, 2008, https://abcnews.go.com/Blotter/De mocraticDebate/story?id=4443788&page=1.

2. See Bryan Burrough, *Days of Rage: America's Radical Underground, the FBI, and the Forgotten Age of Revolutionary Violence* (New York: Penguin Books, 2016), 6. Ayers and Dohrn's violent revolutionary activities are amply documented in this fascinating book.

3. See Roger Kimball, *Tenured Radicals*, 3rd ed. (Chicago: Ivan R. Dee, 2008).

4. Obama's far-left credentials were established by David Freddoso, *The Case Against Barack Obama: The Unlikely Rise and Unexamined Agenda of the Media's Favorite Candidate* (Washington, D.C.: Regnery, 2008). He does not argue that Obama was not born in the United States, nor do I believe it. For the crimes of the Obama administration, see Ben Shapiro, *The People vs. Barack Obama: The Criminal Case Against The Obama Administration* (New York: Threshold Editions, 2015).

5. Francis Schaeffer, *How Should We Then Live?* (Wheaton, IL: Crossway, [1976] 2005), 205.

6. Neil Postman, *Amusing Ourselves to Death: Public Discourse in an Age of Show Business* (New York, Penguin, 1985).

7. Ibid., "Media as Epistemology."

8. See Schaeffer, *How Should We Then Live?*

9. For a helpful guide on news, see Alain de Botton, *The News: A User's Manual* (New York: Pantheon Books, 2014).

10. See Neil Postman and Steve Powers, *How to Watch TV News*, rev. ed. (New York: Penguin, 2008).

11. Nicholas Carr, *The Shallows: What the Internet Is Doing to Our Brains* (New York: W. W. Norton, 2010).

12. See Mark Levin, *Unfreedom of the Press* and Marvin Olasky and Warren Cole Smith, *Prodigal Press,* rev. ed. (Nutley, NJ: P&R, 2013).

13. The very liberal *New York Times,* which sponsored the 1619 Project referred to elsewhere in the book, carries two editorial writers who are mildly conservative on some matters, David Brooks and Ross Douthat.

14. See Mark Levin, *Unfreedom of the Press* (New York: Threshold Editions, 2019).

15. Bruce Bartlett, *The Truth Matters: A Citizen's Guide to Separating Facts from Lies and Stopping Fake News in Its Tracks* (Berkeley: Ten Speed Press, 2017).

16. Daniel Boorstin, *The Image: A Guide to Pseudo Events in America* (New York: Vintage, [1962] 1992).

17. See David Horowitz, *I Can't Breathe: How a Racial Hoax Is Killing America* (Washington, D.C.: Regnery, 2021), 50.

18. George Parry, "Who Killed George Floyd?" *American Spectator,* August 6, 2020, https://spectator.org/george-floyd-death-toxicology-report/; "State of Minnesota v. Derek Michael Chauvin," Prosecutor File No. 20A06620, https://assets.documentcloud.org/documents/6933246/Derek-Chauvin-Co mplaint.pdf.

19. See Horowitz, *I Can't Breathe,* 57–58.

20. All these are Ellison quotes from Mychael Schnell, "Minnesota AG Explains Why Floyd's Death Not Charged as Hate Crime," *The Hill,* April 25, 2021, https://thehill.com/homenews/state-watch/550211-minnesota-ag -explains-why-floyd-death-not-charged-as-hate-crime/.

21. See Bryan Stevenson, *Just Mercy: A Story of Justice and Redemption* (New York: One World, 2014).

22. Horowitz, *I Can't Breathe,* 78.

23. Heather Mac Donald, "Breakdown: The Unwinding of Law and Order in Our Cities Has Happened with Stunning Speed," *City Journal,* July 1, 2020, https://www.city-journal.org/ferguson-effect-inner-cities.

24. Ibid. See Heather Mac Donald, *The War on Cops: How the New Attack on Law and Order Makes Everyone Less Safe* (New York: Encounter Books, 2017).

25. Zusha Elinson, Dan Frosch, and Joshua Jamerson, "Cities Reverse Defunding the Police amidst Rising Crime," *Wall Street Journal*, May 26, 2021, https://www.wsj.com/articles/cities-reverse-defunding-the-police-amid-rising-crime-11622066307.

26. John McWhorter, *Woke Racism* (New York: Penguin Publishing Group, 2021), 146.

27. Ibid., 147.

28. Horowitz, *I Can't Breathe*; Wilfred Reilly, *Hate Crime Hoax: How the Left Is Selling a Fake Race War* (Washington, D.C.: Regnery, 2019).

29. Reilly, *Hate Crime Hoax*, 10.

30. Thomas Sowell, *Barbarians Inside the Gates and Other Controversial Essays* (Stanford, CA: Hoover Institution Press, 1999), 264.

31. R. J. Rushdoony, *Politics of Guilt and Pity* (Vallecito, CA: Chalcedon/Ross House Books, 1970), 17, Kindle.

32. Francis Schaeffer, *True Spirituality* (Carol Stream, IL: Tyndale House Publishers, 1971), 3.

33. *The Gulag Archipelago*, Part 4, Chapter 1, "The Ascent."

34. Rushdoony, *Politics of Guilt and Pity*, 17.

35. Ibid.

36. *APA Dictionary of Psychology*, s.v. "masochism, n.," https://dictionary.apa.org/masochism.

37. Rushdoony, *Politics of Guilt and Pity*, 23.

38. For an excellent summary of Steele's views on race in America, see Samuel Kronen, "American Humanist," *City Journal* (Autumn 2021), https://www.city-journal.org/shelby-steele-american-race-relations.

39. Shelby Steele, *A Dream Deferred* (New York: HarperCollins, 1998), 18.

40. Ibid., 13.

41. Ibid., 39.

42. Ibid., 34.

43. See Shelby Steele, *White Guilt* (New York: HarperCollins, 2006).

44. On Steele's biography and ideas, see Kronen, "American Humanist."

Chapter Three: What Is America, and Should We Burn It?

1. On Antifa, see Andy Ngo, *Unmasked: Inside Antifa's Radical Plan to Destroy Democracy* (New York: Center Street, 2021), and from the pro-Antifa perspective, Mark Bray, *Antifa: The Anti-Fascist Handbook* (Brooklyn, NY: Melville House, 2017).
2. Richard Hofstadter, *Anti-Intellectualism in American Life* (New York: Vintage Books), 145. Hofstadter writes this as part of a lament that America would become anti-intellectual in many aspects of its character.
3. I address the need for civic rituals in Section IV: "A Better Fire."
4. History.com Editors, "Mayflower Compact," September 29, 2009, https://www.history.com/topics/colonial-america/mayflower-compact#section_7.
5. Martin Luther King Jr., "I Have a Dream" speech, Washington, D.C., August 28, 1963, American Rhetoric, http://www.americanrhetoric.com/speeches/mlkihaveadream.htm.
6. Quoted in Os Guinness, *Last Call for Liberty* (Downers Grove, IL: InterVarsity Press, 2018), 19.
7. I owe this turn of phrase to a speech by Rick Santorum.
8. For an in-depth and profound treatment of America as a covenanted nation, see Guinness, *Last Call for Liberty*, 24–28.
9. Zara Anishanslin, "What We Get Wrong about Ben Franklin's 'a Republic, If You Can Keep It,'" *Washington Post*, October 29, 2019, https://www.washingtonpost.com/outlook/2019/10/29/what-we-get-wrong-about-ben-franklins-republic-if-you-can-keep-it. This interesting article highlights the standing and achievements of Mrs. Powel, which are typically forgotten when the exchange is related.
10. "From George Washington to Catharine Sawbridge Macaulay Graham, 9 January 1790," Founders Online, https://founders.archives.gov/documents/Washington/05-04-02-0363.
11. "Address to the New Jersey State Senate," Abraham Lincoln Online, February 21, 1861, http://www.abrahamlincolnonline.org/lincoln/speeches/trenton1.htm. Emphasis added.
12. "Annual Message to Congress: Concluding Remarks," Abraham Lincoln Online, December 1, 1862, http://www.abrahamlincolnonline.org/lincoln/speeches/congress.htm.
13. For a chronology of important dates regarding slavery, including when nations abolished it, see "Who Banned Slavery When?" Reuters, March 22, 2007, https://www.reuters.com/article/uk-slavery/chronology-who-banned-slavery-when-idUSL1561464920070322.

14. The 1619 Project's two other main claims are that Abraham Lincoln was a racist and that the plantation harvesting of cotton was the basis of capitalism in America. I address the critique of capitalism as racist in "Should We Set Flames to the Free Market?" Peter W. Wood refutes the historical claim in *1620: A Critical Response to the 1619 Project* (New York: Encounter Books, 2020), 124–30; 132–43. That Lincoln was a racist is absurd, as will be obvious below. But for the details, see Mary Grabar, "Taking Down Abraham Lincoln" in *Debunking the 1619 Project: Exposing the Plan to Divide America* (Washington D.C.: Regnery History, 2021).

15. The original document can be found at The Pulitzer Center: https://pulitzercenter.org/sites/default/files/full_issue_of_the_1619_project.pdf.

16. Peter Wood, *1620: A Critical Response to the 1619 Project.* (New York: Encounter Books, 2020); Grabar, *Debunking the 1619 Project.* Even a collection of essays mostly from a Trotskyite perspective was released: David North, ed., *The New York Times' 1619 Project and the Racialist Falsification of History* (Royal Oak, MI: Mehring Books, 2021). Trotskyites are Marxists who side with Trotsky over Lenin.

17. Wood, *1620*, 222.

18. Matthew Karp, "History as End: 1619, 1776, and the Politics of the Past," *Harpers*, July 2021, https://harpers.org/archive/2021/07/history-as-end-politics-of-the-past-matthew-karp.

19. Charles Kessler, "Call Them the 1619 Riots," *New York Post*, June 19, 2020, https://nypost.com/2020/06/19/call-them-the-1619-riots.

20. Virginia Allen, "*New York Times* Mum on '1619 Project' Creator Calling '1619 Riots' Moniker an 'Honor,'" *Daily Signal*, June 22, 2020, https://www.dailysignal.com/2020/06/22/new-york-times-mum-on-1619-project-creator-calling-1619-riots-moniker-an-honor/. This, by implication, places Ms. Hannah-Jones in the same camp as Marxist-Anarchist Vicky Osterweil, *In Defense of Looting* (New York: Bold Type Books, 2020).

21. Nikole Hannah-Jones et al., *The 1619 Project: A New Origins Story* (New York: One World Books, 2021). The book came out after I had written the substance of this book, so I could not engage it in detail. I hope to in a future book, however.

22. See Robert Woodson's review of *The 1619 Project* book at *Daily Mail*, November 22, 2021, https://www.dailymail.co.uk/news/article-10231195/The-Continued-Failure-1619-Project-New-Origin-Civil-Rights-Activist-Bob-Woodson.html.

23. "The Declaration of Independence," National Archives, https://www.arc hives.gov/founding-docs/declaration-transcript. The spelling reproduces that of the original document.

24. The Declaration did not endorse hedonism. To the Founders, *happiness* essentially meant *virtue* or *human flourishing*. This trades on the classic Greek and Christian understanding of *happiness*, not the modern view.

25. Larry P. Arnn, Carol Swain, and Matthew Spalding, *The 1776 Report* (New York: Encounter Books, 2021), 10.

26. Ibid., 30–31.

27. Ibid., 28.

28. "Jefferson's Notes on Slavery," American History, https://www.let.rug.nl /usa/documents/1776-1785/jeffersons-notes-on-slavery.php. Emphasis added.

29. James Oakes, *The Crooked Path to Abolition: Abraham Lincoln and the Antislavery Constitution* (New York: W. W. Norton & Company), xv–xvi.

30. Frederick Douglass, *The Portable Frederick Douglass* (New York: Penguin Books, 2016), 200. All boldface in the original.

31. "Transcript of the Proclamation," National Archives, https://www.archiv es.gov/exhibits/featured-documents/emancipation-proclamation/transcri pt.html.

32. For a particular example of the cruel and unjust Jim Crow South, see Keisha N. Blain, *Until I Am Free: Fannie Lou Hamer's Enduring Message to America* (New York: Beacon Press, 2021). Also, listen to Fannie Lou Hamer's nine-minute testimony of being beaten for registering to vote at the 1965 Democratic Convention: Fascinating LiiFe, "1964 Full Speech Fannie Lou Hamer Voice of Freedom," YouTube, June 18, 2020, https:// www.youtube.com/watch?v=RobTthUg04c.

33. Martin Luther King Jr., "I Have a Dream" speech, Washington, D.C., August 28, 1963, American Rhetoric, http://www.americanrhetoric .com/speeches/mlkihaveadream.htm.

34. Blain, *Until I Am Free.*

35. Robert Goldwin, "Why Blacks, Women, and Jews Are Not Mentioned in the Constitution," *Commentary*, May 1987, https://www.commentary.org /articles/robert-goldwin/why-blacks-women-jews-are-not-mentioned-in-the -constitution.

36. "Madison Debates: https://avalon.law.yale.edu/18th_century/debates_825 .asp. See also Sean Wilentz, *No Property in Man: Slavery and Anti-Slavery*

at the Nation's Founding (Cambridge, MA: Harvard University Press, 2018), iii.

37. "Constitution of the Confederate States; March 11, 1861," The Avalon Project, https://avalon.law.yale.edu/19th_century/csa_csa.asp.

38. Goldwin, "Why Blacks, Women, and Jews are Not Mentioned in the Constitution."

39. Ibid.

40. Ibid.

41. Ibid.

42. Paul Johnson, *A History of the American People* (New York: HarperCollins, 1997), 316.

43. On Douglass's change of mind, see David W. Blight, "My Faithful Friend Julia" in *Frederick Douglass: Prophet of Freedom* (New York: Simon and Schuster, 2018).

44. Ibid., 13.

45. Ibid.

46. Ibid.

47. Timothy Sandefur, *The Conscience of the Constitution: The Declaration of Independence and the Right to Liberty* (Washington, D.C.: Cato Institute, 2015).

48. Oakes, *The Crooked Path to Abolition.*

49. Shelby Steele, *Shame: How America's Past Sins Have Polarized Our Country* (New York: Basic Books, 2015), 198.

50. See Carol Swain, *The New White Nationalism In America: Its Challenge to Integration* (New York: Cambridge University Press, 2004).

51. Ariel Zilber, "Whoops!...," *Daily Mail,* October 31, 2021, https://www.dailymail.co.uk/news/article-10150967/Ibram-X-Kendi-deletes-tweet-white-college-applicants-LIE-black.html.

52. "34% of White College Students Lied about Their Race to Improve Chances of Admission, Financial Aid Benefits," Intelligent, https://www.intelligent.com/34-of-white-college-students-lied-about-their-race-to-improve-chances-of-admission-financial-aid-benefits/.

53. "Talking about Race: Whiteness," National Museum of African American History and Culture, https://nmaahc.si.edu/learn/talking-about-race/topics/whiteness.

54. See Charles Murray, *American Exceptionalism: An Experiment in History* (Washington, D.C.: AEI Press, 2013); Seymour Martin Lipset, *American Exceptionalism: A Double-Edged Sword* (New York: W. W. Norton,

1996); Os Guinness, *The Great Experiment: Faith and Freedom in America* (Colorado Springs, CO: NavPress, 2001).
55. See John Pitney, "The Tocqueville Fraud," *Washington Examiner*, November 12, 1995, https://www.washingtonexaminer.com/weekly-stan dard/the-tocqueville-fraud.

Chapter Four: America and Systemic Racism

1. Ibram X. Kendi, *How to Be an Antiracist* (New York: Random House, 2019), 19.
2. See Senator Josh Hawley's excellent statement on Critical Race Theory and Kendi's ideas: Forbes Breaking News, "Josh Hawley Attacks Teachings of Dr. Ibram X. Kendi, Critical Race Theory in Senate Floor Speech," YouTube, June 22, 2021, https://www.youtube.com/watch?v=aTzMooZ Nwbs.
3. Ibram X. Kendi, "Pass an Anti-Racist Constitutional Amendment," *Politico*, https://www.politico.com/interactives/2019/how-to-fix-politics -in-america/inequality/pass-an-anti-racist-constitutional-amendment.
4. Thomas Sowell, *Discrimination and Disparities* (New York: Basic Books, 2018), 22. See Fernand Braudel, *A History of Civilizations*, translated by Richard Mayne (New York: Penguin Press, 1994), 17; and Donald L. Horowitz, *Ethnic Groups in Conflict* (Berkeley: University of California Press, 1985), 677. Sowell has argued for this through many of his books.
5. For an inside account of the revolutionary and violent nature of the Black Panthers, see David Horowitz, *Hating Whitey and Other Progressive Causes* (Spence Publishing Company, 1999).
6. Horowitz, *Hating Whitey and Other Progressive Causes*, 82.
7. Robin DiAngelo, *White Fragility* (New York: Beacon Press, 2020).
8. Ibram X. Kendi, "My Racist Introduction," in *How to Be an Antiracist* (New York: Random House, 2019).
9. Quoted in Kendi, *How to Be an Antiracist*, 46. Kendi does not use the term anymore, but speaks rather of "racist abuse," rather than "micro-aggression."
10. John McWhorter discusses this in *Woke Racism* (New York: Penguin Publishing Group, 2021), 160–67.
11. See Douglas Groothuis, *Truth Decay: Defending Christianity Against the Challenge of Postmodernism* (Downers Grove, IL: InterVarsity Press, 2000), 98–100.

12. "Talking about Race: Whiteness," National Museum of African American History and Culture, https://nmaahc.si.edu/learn/talking-about-race/topics/whiteness.

13. Ibid.

14. On the troubles of Appalachia, see the bestselling memoir, J. D. Vance, *Hillbilly Elegy: A Memoir of a Family and Culture in Crisis* (New York: Harper, 2016). This was also made into a film in 2020.

15. Abby Budiman, "Indians in the U.S. Fact Sheet," Pew Research Center, April 29, 2021, https://www.pewresearch.org/social-trends/fact-sheet/asian-americans-indians-in-the-u-s.

16. "Median Household Income in the United States in 2020, by Race or Ethnic Group," Statista, https://www.statista.com/statistics/233324/median-household-income-in-the-united-states-by-race-or-ethnic-group.

17. On the Ku Klux Klan, see David M. Chalmers, *Hooded Americanism: The History of the Ku Klux Klan* (Durham, NC: Duke University Press, 1987).

18. See "Alt Right: A Primer on the New White Supremacy," Anti-Defamation League, https://www.adl.org/resources/backgrounders/alt-right-a-primer-on-the-new-white-supremacy.

19. Sowell, *Discrimination and Disparities*, 117.

20. "Obama's Father's Day Remarks: Transcript," *New York Times*, June 15, 2008, https://www.nytimes.com/2008/06/15/us/politics/15text-obama.html.

21. Fatherhood in general has suffered a loss of meaning. See David Blankenhorn, *Fatherless America: Confronting Our Most Urgent Social Problem* (New York: Harper, 1995).

22. Kay S. Hymowitz, "The Black Family: 40 Years of Lies," *City Journal* (Summer 2005), https://www.city-journal.org/html/black-family-40-years-lies-12872.html.

23. This is the view of the black conversative and ex-welfare recipient, Star Parker, in *White Ghetto: How Middle Class America Reflects Inner City Decay* (Nashville, TN: Thomas Nelson, 2009).

24. Thomas Sowell, "A Legacy of Liberalism," Creator's Syndicate, November 18, 2014, https://www.creators.com/read/thomas-sowell/11/14/a-legacy-of-liberalism.

25. See Thomas Sowell, "The Special Case of Blacks" in *Civil Rights: Rhetoric or Reality?* (New York: William Morrow, 1984). Sowell's views on culture are ably summarized and referenced in Jason Reilly, "Culture Matters" in

Maverick: A Biography of Thomas Sowell (New York: Basic Books, 2021). This is a stellar intellectual biography.

26. Thomas Sowell, *Preferential Policies* (New York: William Morrow, 1990), 149.

27. See Thomas Sowell, "The Overseas Chinese" in *The Politics and Economics of Race* (New York: William Morrow, 1983).

28. Shelby Steele, "The Loneliness of the Black Conservative" in *A Dream Deferred: The Second Betrayal of Black Freedom in America* (New York: Harper Perennial, 1999).

29. Kendi, *How to Be an Antiracist*, 153.

30. Thomas Sowell, *The Vision of the Anointed: Self-Congratulation as a Basis for Social Policy* (New York: Basic Books, 1995), 198.

31. Ibid.

32. Ibid.

33. Ibid., 200.

34. Katherine Schaeffer, "The Most Common Age among Whites in U.S. is 58—More than Double That of Racial and Ethnic Minorities," Pew Research Center, July 30, 2019, https://www.pewresearch.org/fact-tank/2019/07/30/most-common-age-among-us-racial-ethnic-groups. Note: "most common age" is the *mode* measurement (the most frequently occurring value on the list); *median* is the average age of all in a category.

35. Sowell, *Discrimination and Disparities*, 24–25.

36. See Charles Murray, "Part 1: A Generous Revolution" in *Losing Ground: American Social Policy, 1950–1980* (New York: Basic Books, [1984] 2015).

37. Murray, *Losing Ground*, 14.

38. This is documented extensively in Murray.

39. Marvin Olasky argues that the modern welfare state mentality is deleterious to the poor and differs crucially from historical American approaches to poverty, which stressed individual responsibility and uplift. See *The Tragedy of American Compassion* (Washington, D.C.: Regnery, 1994).

40. Jason Riley, *Please Stop Helping Us: How Liberals Make it Harder for Blacks to Succeed* (New York: Encounter Books, 2016). See also Jason Riley, *False Black Power* (Chicago: Templeton Press, 2017); Candace Owens, *Blackout* (New York: Threshold Editions, 2020).

41. Amy Wax, *Rights, Wrongs, and Remedies: Group Justice in the 21st Century* (Lanham, MD: Rowman and Littlefield, 2009), 14–17, cited in Coleman Huges, "Black American Culture and the Racial Wealth Gap,"

Quillette, July 19, 2018, https://quillette.com/2018/07/19/black-american
-culture-and-the-racial-wealth-gap.

42. Derrick Bell, *Faces at the Bottom of the Well: The Permanence of Racism*
(New York: Basic Books, [1992] 2018).

43. Derrick Bell, *Silent Covenants* (Oxford University Press, 2004), 49.

44. Bell, "The Space Traders" in *Faces at the Bottom of the Well.*

45. Michelle Alexander, "Foreword" in *Faces at the Bottom of the Well*, xvii.

46. I addressed the idea of objectivity or neutrality in Chapter Five: "Ideology
and Torching Free Speech."

47. Shelby Steele interview on C-SPAN, quoted in Samuel Kronen, "An
American Humanist," *City Journal* (Autumn 2021).

48. Thomas Chatterton Williams, "How Ta-Nehisi Coates Gives Whiteness
Power," *New York Times*, October 6, 2017, https://www.nytimes.com/20
17/10/06/opinion/ta-nehisi-coates-whiteness-power.html.

49. Michelle Alexander concurs in her foreword to *Faces at the Bottom of the
Well.*

50. Thomas Sowell, *Civil Rights* (New York: HarperCollins, 1984), 39.

51. Seymour Martin Lipset, *American Exceptionalism: A Double-Edged
Sword* (New York: W. W. Norton, 1996), 120.

52. Ibid., 119.

53. Kenny Xu, *An Inconvenient Minority: The Attack on Asian American
Excellence and the Fight for Meritocracy* (New York: Diversion Books,
2021).

54. Ibid., 3.

55. Ibid., 4.

56. See Mike Gonzalez, *The Plot to Change America: How Identity Politics
Is Dividing the Land of the Free* (New York: Encounter Books, 2020).

57. Shelby Steele, *The Content of Our Character* (New York: Harper Perennial,
1990), 115–18.

58. Seymour Martin Lipset writes of Frederick Douglass's opposition to quotas
for black people in *American Exceptionalism: A Double-Edged Sword*
(New York: W. W. Norton, 1996), 148.

59. Dinesh D'Souza, "More Equal Than Others" in *Illiberal Education:
Political Correctness and Liberal Education* (New York: Free Press, 1992).
During a faculty meeting in the mid-1990s, I pointed out his conclusions
about the adverse effects of preferential admission policies and was called
a racist by a colleague. But *facts* cannot be racist.

60. Thomas Sowell, "Affirmative Action around the World," *Hoover Digest* 2004, no. 4 (October 30, 2004), https://www.hoover.org/research/affirmative-action-around-world; and, in more detail, Thomas Sowell, *Affirmative Action Around the World: An Empirical Study* (New Haven, CT: Yale University Press, 2005).
61. Heather Mac Donald, *The Diversity Delusion: How Race and Gender Pandering Corrupt the University and Undermine Our Culture* (New York: St. Martin's Press, 2018).
62. Richard Sander and Stuart Taylor Jr., *Mismatch* (New York: Basic Books, 2012). See also Xu, *An Inconvenient Minority.*
63. Steele, *The Content of Our Character*, 116.

Chapter Five: Ideology and Torching Free Speech
1. George Orwell, *1984* (New York: Signet, [1949] 1977), 249.
2. Ibid.
3. On this theme, see the important book by Rod Dreher, *Live Not by Lies: A Manual for Christian Dissidents* (New York: Sentinel, 2020). For faithful living in a time of social decay, see also Rod Dreher, *The Benedict Option: A Strategy for Christians in a Post-Christian Nation* (New York: Sentinel, 2017).
4. For example, Charles Murray uses the term "ideology" to refer to America's founding philosophy without anything derogatory assumed by the term in *American Exceptionalism.*
5. Russell Kirk, "The Poison of Ideology," in *The Essential Russell Kirk: Selected Essays*, ed. George A. Panichas (Wilmington, DE: Intercollegiate Studies Institute, 2006).
6. Kenneth Minogue, *Alien Powers: The Pure Theory of Ideology* (New Brunswick, NJ: Transaction Publishers, 2007).
7. See Charles Murray, *Losing Ground: American Social Policy, 1950–80* (New York: Basic Books, [1984] 2016).
8. See my discussion in Chapter Two: "Fire in Our Own House."
9. Henry Giniger, "Sartre Is Arrested at Last, but Briefly, for Role on a Maoist Weekly," *New York Times*, June 27, 1970, https://www.nytimes.com/1970/06/27/archives/sartre-is-arrested-at-last-but-briefly-for-role-on-a-maoist-weekly.html. The newspaper Sartre was promoting was calling for violence against the French government.

10. This was Mao's movement (also known as the Great Purge) to purge China of opposition, vanquish his adversaries, counter "bureaucratism," and create yet another new society. See Valerie Strauss and Daniel Southerl, "How Many Died? New Evidence Suggests Far Higher Numbers For the Victims of Mao Zedong's Era," *Washington Post*, July 17, 1994, https://www.washingtonpost.com/archive/politics/1994/07/17/how-many-died-new-evidence-suggests-far-higher-numbers-for-the-victims-of-mao-zedongs-era/01044df5-03dd-49f4-a453-a033c5287bce.

11. See my discussion of the media in Chapter Two: "Fire in Our Own House."

12. Minogue, *Alien Powers*, 3. This is the definitive study of ideology.

13. Ludwig von Mises, *Marxism Unmasked* (Irvington, NY: Foundation for Economic Education, 2006), 29.

14. Philosopher Eric Voegelin advanced this thesis in several books, such as *The New Science of Politics* (Chicago: University of Chicago Press, 1987). See also Benjamin Wiker, "The New Science of Politics," in *Ten Books Every Conservative Should Read: Plus Four Not to Miss and One Imposter* (Washington, D.C.: Regnery, 2010).

15. David Horowitz, *Hating Whitey and Other Progressive Causes* (Spence Publishing Company, 1999).

16. Peter Berger and Anton Zijderveld, *In Praise of Doubt: How to Have Convictions Without Becoming a Fanatic* (New York: HarperOne, 2009), 57; see 57–68 for the full discussion.

17. On the role of left-wing or progressive ideology in the development of public education in America, see R. J. Rushdoony, *The Messianic Character of American Education* (Vallecito, CA: Ross House Books, 1995). On the general malaise in public education, see Thomas Sowell, *Inside American Education: The Decline, the Dogmas, the Deception* (New York: Free Press, 1992). Mark Levin discusses the progressivist (or far-left) goals of many educators (especially John Dewey) in "Hate America, Inc." in *American Marxism* (New York: Threshold Editions, 2021).

18. Herbert Marcuse, "Repressive Tolerance," https://www.marcuse.org/herbert/publications/1960s/1965-repressive-tolerance-fulltext.html.

19. Mark Bray, *Antifa: The Anti-Fascist Handbook* (Brooklyn: Melville House, 2017), xv.

20. See Andy Ngo, *Unmasked: Inside Antifa's Radical Plan to Destroy Democracy* (Nashville, TN: Center Street, 2021). The 2021 Western Conservative Summit was disrupted by Antifa protests, sparked by the

appearance of Andy Ngo, who has been repeatedly assaulted by Antifa members.

21. *No Safe Spaces*, directed by Justin Folk, featuring Dennis Prager and Adam Carolla (Atlas Distribution Company, 2019), https://nosafespaces.com. This episode begins at 49 minutes. See also Dennis Prager and Mark Joseph, eds., "Showing Up For Work Is the New Racism," in *No Safe Spaces* (Washington, D.C.: Regnery, 2019). The book reports many cases where free speech was stymied.

22. Prager and Joseph, eds., *No Safe Spaces*, 7.

23. Abby Spegman, "Evergreen Professor at Heart of Controversy Resigns; Receives $500,000," *Seattle Times*, September 16, 2017, https://www.sea ttletimes.com/seattle-news/evergreen-professor-at-center-of-protests-resig ns-college-will-pay-500000.

24. Bari Weiss, "When the Left Turns on Its Own" *New York Times*, June 1, 2017, https://www.nytimes.com/2017/06/01/opinion/when-the-left-turns -on-its-own.html?smid=tw-share. Weiss later resigned from the *New York Times* because of its unethical practices. Her letter can be found here: https://www.bariweiss.com/resignation-letter.

25. Brittany Bernstein, "UNC Dean Worried 'Diversity of Thought' Would Interfere with Social Justice ahead of Nikole Hannah-Jones Appointment," *National Review*, August 9, 2021, https://www.nationalreview.com/news /unc-dean-worried-diversity-of-thought-would-interfere-with-social-justi ce-ahead-of-nikole-hannah-jones-appointment/.

26. See Sara Atske et al., "Seven Facts about Black Americans and the New Media," Pew Research Center, August 7, 2019, https://www.pewresearch .org/fact-tank/2019/08/07/facts-about-black-americans-and-the-news -media. Point seven addresses black representation in various aspects of media, which show some disparities of representation from the overall population, but nothing warranting the suspension of free speech, since free speech is a key factor which has helped black people advance and which would continue to serve that end.

27. Chris Demaske, "Critical Race Theory," *First Amendment Encyclopedia*, https://www.mtsu.edu/first-amendment/article/1254/critical-race-theory.

28. Ibid.

29. Ibram X. Kendi, "When Free Speech Becomes Unfree Speech," Diverse Education, https://diverseeducation.com/article/78479.

30. John R. Vile, "Campus Speech Codes," *First Amendment Encyclopedia,* https://mtsu.edu/first-amendment/article/991/campus-speech-codes.

31. Ibid.

32. Quoted in Nadine Strossen, "Counterspeech as a Response to Changing Notions of Free Speech," *Human Rights* 33, no. 4 (October 2018), https://www.americanbar.org/groups/crsj/publications/human_rights_magazine_home/the-ongoing-challenge-to-define-free-speech/counterspeech-in-response-to-free-speech.

33. Oliver Wendell Holmes, *Abrams v. United States* 250 U.S. 616 (1919), Dissenting Opinion by Justice Holmes, University of Baltimore, https://home.ubalt.edu/id86mp66/Class%20Reference/Incitement/Abrams_dissent.htm.

34. Louis D. Brandeis, "Chapter V: What Publicity Can Do" in *Other People's Money*, https://louisville.edu/law/library/special-collections/the-louis-d.-brandeis-collection/other-peoples-money-chapter-v.

35. John Stuart Mill, *On Liberty* (Mineola, NY: Dover Publications, 2002), 30.

36. Ibid., 14.

37. Plato, *Gorgias* of *Plato in Twelve Volumes*, vol. 3, trans. W. R. M. Lam (Cambridge, MA: Harvard University Press, 1967), 458a, Perseus Digital Library, http://www.perseus.tufts.edu/hopper/text?doc=urn:cts:greekLit:tlg0059.tlg023.perseus-eng1:458a.

38. DiAngelo refers to "implicit bias" six times in *White Fragility*, but gives no sustained defense of the concept. Robin DiAngelo, *White Fragility* (New York: Beacon Press, 2018), xiii, 43, 45, 81, 126, 163. For an academic critique of implicit bias, see Bertram Gawronski, "Six Lessons for a Cogent Science of Implicit Bias and Its Criticism," *Perspectives on Psychological Science* 14, no. 4 (July 2019): 574–95, https://doi.org/10.1177/1745691619826015.

39. Karl Marx, *The Communist Manifesto* (Lawrence, KS: Neeland Media, [1848] 2017), 16.

40. "Cognitive access to reality" is a term for knowledge coined by philosopher, Linda Zagzebski.

41. Richard Delgado and Jean Stefancic, *Introducing Critical Race Theory*, 3rd ed. (New York: New York University Press, 2017), 12–13.

42. J. P. Moreland, *Love Your God with All Your Mind: The Role of Reason in the Life of the Soul*, 2nd ed. (Colorado Springs, CO: NavPress, [1997] 2012), 116.

43. Susan Svrluga, "UC-Berkeley Braced for Protests When Conservative Writer Ben Shapiro Came to Campus," *Washington Post*, September 15,

2017, https://www.washingtonpost.com/news/grade-point/wp/2017/09/14
/uc-berkeley-braces-for-protests-as-conservative-writer-ben-shapiro-spea
ks-on-campus.

Chapter Six: Shall We Set Flames to the Free Market?

1. Tonya Mosley, "'An Extraordinary Moment': Angela Davis Says Protests Recognize Long Overdue Anti-Racist Work," *Here and Now*, WBUR, June 19, 2020, https://www.wbur.org/hereandnow/2020/06/19/angela-da vis-protests-anti-racism. Lest the reader think I am calling names, Angela Davis has self-identified as a "communist" since the 1960s.
2. Marian Tupy, "Anti-Racists Should Think Twice about Allying with Socialism," November 14, 2017, Foundation for Economic Freedom, https://fee.org/articles/anti-racists-should-think-twice-about-allying-with -socialism/.
3. Interview with Ibram X. Kendi, "*How to Be an Antiracist* Author Ibram X. Kendi on What We Get Wrong about Racism," *TIME*, August 8, 2019, https://time.com/5647303/how-to-be-antiracist-author-interview.
4. Ibram X. Kendi, *How to Be an Antiracist* (New York: Random House, 2019), 158.
5. Tupy, "Anti-Racists Should Think Twice about Allying with Socialism."
6. "Black Lives Matter . . . What We Believe," University of Central Arkansas, https://uca.edu/training/files/2020/09/black-Lives-Matter-Handout.pdf. This statement was later taken off their web page for purposes of camouflage, not because of a change of mind.
7. See William Bennett, *The Broken Hearth: Reversing the Moral Collapse of the American Family* (New York: Crown Publishing, [2001] 2003).
8. Thomas Sowell, *Discrimination and Disparities* (New York: Basic Books, 2018), 219–20.
9. Chelsea Patterson Sobolik and Michael Sobolik, "How the Chinese Communist Party Is Persecuting the Uyghur Muslims," Ethics and Religious Liberty Commission, August 17, 2020, https://erlc.com/resource -library/articles/how-the-chinese-communist-party-is-persecuting-uyghur -muslims.
10. See Dinesh D'Souza, "The American Dilemma: Was Slavery a Racist Institution?" in *The End of Racism: Principles for a Multiracial Society* (New York: Free Press, 1995).

11. Thomas Sowell, *Black Rednecks and White Liberals* (San Francisco: Encounter Books, 2005), 127.

12. Joseph L. Bast, *Education and Capitalism* (Stanford, CA: Hoover Institution Press, 2003), 132.

13. Thomas Sowell, "The Economics of Slavery" in *Markets and Minorities* (New York: Basic Books, 1981).

14. Ibid., 100–101.

15. Ibid., 101.

16. Bast, *Education and Capitalism*, 134.

17. William Julius Wilson, *The Declining Significance of Race* (University of Chicago Press, 1980), 147; quoted in Joseph L. Bast, *Education and Capitalism* (Stanford, CA: Hoover Institution Press, 2003), 134–35.

18. Richard Rothstein, interview by Terry Gross, "A 'Forgotten History' of How the U.S. Government Segregated America," *Fresh Air*, NPR, May 3, 2017, https://www.npr.org/2017/05/03/526655831/a-forgotten-history-of -how-the-u-s-government-segregated-america. Richard Rothstein is the author of *The Color of Law: A Forgotten History of How Our Government Segregated America* (New York: Liveright, 2018).

19. Sowell, *Discrimination and Disparities*, 45–46.

20. See Walter E. Williams, *South Africa's War on Capitalism* (New York: Prager, 1989).

21. Adam Smith, *The Wealth of Nations* (Lulu Press, [1776] 2016), eBook, https://www.lulu.com/en/us/shop/adam-smith/the-wealth-of-nations/ebo ok/product-1djv6ynd.html?page=1&pageSize=4.

22. "Joe, the Plumber, Happy to Help Candidates Make Point," CNN, https:// www.cnn.com/2008/POLITICS/10/16/joe.plumber/index.html.

23. Thomas Sowell, *Basic Economics* (New York: Basic Books, 2004), 16–18.

24. Ibid., 631.

25. On this general problem, see Thomas Sowell, *The Vision of the Anointed: Self-Congratulation as a Basis for Social Policy* (New York: Basic Books, 1996) and *The Quest for Cosmic Justice* (New York: Free Press, 1999).

26. Sowell, *The Quest for Cosmic Justice*.

27. Rand Paul, *The Case Against Socialism* (New York: Broadside Books, 2019), 9. See the chapter "Socialism Destroyed Venezuela's Once Vibrant Economy."

28. Luka Ladan, "Capitalism Remains the Best Way to Alleviate Extreme Poverty," Catalyst, June 14, 2019, https://catalyst.independent.org/2019 /06/14/capitalism-remains-the-best-way-to-combat-extreme-poverty.

29. Michael Rectenwald, *Springtime for Snowflakes: Social Justice and Its Postmodern Parentage* (Nashville: New English Review Press, 2018), 113.

30. Milton Friedman, "Capitalism and Freedom" in *New Individualist Review* (Indianapolis: Liberty Fund, 1981), Online Library of Liberty, https://oll.li bertyfund.org/page/friedman-on-capitalism-and-freedom.

31. Editors of Encyclopaedia Britannica, "New Economic Policy," *Encyclopaedia Britannica*, May 22, 2020, https://www.britannica.com/ev ent/New-Economic-Policy-Soviet-history.

32. For the socialist trend in contemporary American politics, see Dinesh D'Souza, *The United States of Socialism* (New York: All Points Books, 2020); Mark Levine, *American Marxism* (New York: Threshold Editions, 2021).

33. Sowell, *Basic Economics*, 220–21.

34. Ibid, 223.

35. Ibid, 224.

36. See Sowell's chapter "Minimum Wage Laws" in *Basic Economics*. See also Walter Williams, "Race and Wage Regulation" in *Race and Economics: How Much Can Be Blamed on Discrimination?* (Hoover Institution Press, 2011).

37. Sowell, *Basic Economics*, 451.

38. For more on this, see Jay W. Richards, "Doesn't the Free Market Foster Unfair Competition? Myth No. 3: The Zero-Sum Game Myth," in *Money, Greed, and God: The Christian Case for Free Enterprise*, 10th anniversary ed. (New York: HarperOne, 2019).

39. Harry Frankfurt, *On Inequality* (New Jersey: Princeton University Press, 2015), 46.

40. Ibid.

41. See Helmut Schoeck, *Envy: A Theory of Social Behavior* (Indianapolis: Liberty Press, 1969), 297–300.

42. R. J. Rushdoony, *Politics of Guilt & Pity* (Vallecito, CA: Chalcedon/Ross House Books, 1970), 151–53.

43. Rhoda E. Howard-Hassmann, "Why Japanese Americans Received Reparations and African Americans Are Still Waiting," The Conversation, July 17, 2019, https://theconversation.com/why-japanese-americans-recei ved-reparations-and-african-americans-are-still-waiting-119580.

44. Ibid.

45. Vic Rosenthal and Scott Russell, "Holocaust Survivors Continue to Receive German Reparations Payments to This Day," Healing Minnesota Stories,

February 18, 2021, https://healingmnstories.wordpress.com/2021/02/18/holocaust-survivors-continue-to-receive-german-reparations-payments-to-this-day.

46. Ta-Nehisi Coates, "The Case for Reparations," *Atlantic*, June 2014, https://www.theatlantic.com/magazine/archive/2014/06/the-case-for-reparations/361631.

47. Adam Hayes, "Redlining," Investopedia, October 21, 2021, https://www.investopedia.com/terms/r/redlining.asp.

48. I address this is in more depth in Chapter Four: "America and Systemic Racism."

49. I discussed white guilt and white privilege in Chapter Four: "America and Systemic Racism."

50. All of Ezekiel 18 makes this point of individual culpability. While the Message paraphrase is not always accurate, it is in this case.

51. See Tunku Varadarajan, "For Winsome Sears, Education Is Key to Black Success," *Wall Street Journal*, January 7, 2022, https://www.wsj.com/articles/winsome-sears-education-key-black-success-virginia-governor-charter-school-choice-crt-critical-race-theory-11641574129.

52. See Jenna Ross, "Ranked: The World's Black Billionaires in 2021," Visual Capitalist, February 26, 2021, https://www.visualcapitalist.com/black-billionaires-in-2021. The article claims that black people make up only 1 percent of the world's billionaires.

53. Ta-Nehisi Coates, *Between the World and Me* (New York: Spiegel and Grau, 2015).

54. Coates, "The Case for Reparations."

55. See R. J. Rushdoony, *Larceny in the Heart: The Economics of Satan and the Inflationary State* (Vallecito, CA: Ross House Books, [1981] 2002).

56. See the US Debt Clock, which gives an up-to-the-second account of the various aspects of US debt: https://www.usdebtclock.org

57. "The National Debt Explained," Investopedia, February 7, 2022, https://www.investopedia.com/updates/usa-national-debt.

Chapter Seven: Race and Identity

1. Kirk Johnson, Richard Pérez-Peña, and John Eligon, "Rachel Dolezal, in Center of Storm, Is Defiant: 'I Identify as Black'," *New York Times*, June 16, 2015, https://www.nytimes.com/2015/06/17/us/rachel-dolezal-nbc-to

day-show.html. show.html?action=click&module=RelatedCoverage&pgt ype=Article&region=Footer.

2. See Francis Schaeffer, *Genesis in Space and Time* (Downers Grove, IL: InterVarsity Press, 1972).

3. Shelby Steele, *A Bound Man: Why We Are Excited About Obama and Why He Can't Win* (New York: Free Press, 2008), 9–10.

4. James Baldwin, *The Fire Next Time* (New York: Vintage, [1961] 1991), 36. Baldwin's rejection of Christianity makes for sad reading.

5. Ibram X. Kendi, *How to Be an Antiracist* (New York: Random House, 2019), 50–53.

6. For a thorough discussion of this, see C. Herbert Oliver, "The Significance of Shem, Ham, and Japheth" and "The Biblical History of Shem, Ham, and Japheth" in *No Flesh Shall Glory: How the Bible Destroys the Foundations of Racism*, 2nd ed. (Phillipsburg, NJ: P&R Publishing, [1959] 2021).

7. This paragraph is adapted from Douglas Groothuis, *Christian Apologetics: A Comprehensive Case for Biblical Faith*, 2nd ed. (Downers Grove, IL: InterVarsity Academic, 2022), 102–3.

8. Oliver, *No Flesh May Glory*, 27. See his chapter, "The Bible and Color."

9. See Douglas Groothuis, "Jesus' View of Women" in *On Jesus* (Belmont, CA: Wadsworth, 2003).

10. The previous three paragraphs are adapted from Groothuis, *On Jesus* (Belmont, CA: Wadsworth, 2003).

11. The account is found in Mark 7:24–30 and Mathew 15:21–29. I will combine both accounts for the fuller harmony. There are no discrepant elements, but each gospel gives some details not found in the other.

12. I owe this insight to Professor Craig L. Blomberg.

13. On the history of interracial marriage in America, see Jessica Viñas-Nelson, "Interracial Marriage in 'Post-Racial' America," Origins, July 2017, https:// origins.osu.edu/article/interracial-marriage-post-racial-america.

14. For some sound insights on the ontological status of race for blacks, see Victor Anderson, *Beyond Ontological Blackness* (New York: Continuum, 1995).

15. Oliver, *No Flesh May Glory*, 96–97.

16. Ibid., 99.

17. Gretchen Livingston and Anna Brown, "Trends and Patterns in Intermarriage," Pew Research Center, May 18, 2017, https://www.pewre

search.org/social-trends/2017/05/18/1-trends-and-patterns-in-intermarr
iage.

18. Ibid.

19. Gretchen Livingston and Anna Brown, "Public Views on Intermarriage,"
Pew Research Center, May 18, 2017, https://www.pewresearch.org/social
-trends/2017/05/18/2-public-views-on-intermarriage/#fn-22849-10.

20. Ibid.

21. See C. Herbert Oliver, "Human Marriage" in *No Flesh May Glory.*

22. See Craig Keener and Glenn Usry, "A Black Religion: What Do You Say
When Someone Claims That Christianity Is a White Religion?" in
*Defending Black Faith: Answers to Tough Questions About African-
American Christianity* (Downers Grove, IL: InterVarsity Press, 1997).

23. Frederick Douglass, *The Portable Frederick Douglass* (New York: Penguin
Books, 2016), 94.

24. Philip Jenkins, *The Lost History of Christianity: The Thousand-Year
Golden Age of the Church in the Middle East, Africa, and Asia—and
How It Died* (New York: HarperOne, 2008).

25. See Harold Netland's discussion of colonialism and Christian missions in
India in *Christianity and Religious Diversity* (Grand Rapids, MI: Baker
Academic, 2015), 105–7; Douglas Groothuis, "Distortions of Christianity"
in *Christian Apologetics: A Comprehensive Case for Biblical Faith,* 2nd
ed. (Downers Grove, IL: IVP Academic, 2022).

26. Philip Jenkins, *The Next Christendom,* 3rd ed. (New York: Oxford
University Press, 2011).

27. Ruth Tucker, "Colorizing Church History," *Christianity Today,* July 20,
1992, 20.

28. Ibid., 22.

29. See Wayne E. Croft Sr., "John Jasper: Preaching with Authority," Preaching.
com, https://www.preaching.com/articles/past-masters/john-jasper-preac
hing-with-authority.

30. See Charles W. Forman, "Occom, Samson," in *Biographical Dictionary
of Christian Missions,* ed. Gerald H. Anderson (New York: Macmillan
Reference USA, 1998), 503.

31. Ruth Tucker, "Colorizing Church History," 23.

32. Ibid., 23.

33. Ibid., 23. The material from Tucker has been adapted from Douglas
Groothuis, *Truth Decay: Defending Christianity Against the Challenges*

of Postmodernism (Downers Grove, IL: InterVarsity Press, 2000), 220–22.

34. E. V. Hill, *A Savior Worth Having* (Chicago: Moody Publishers, 2002).

35. For more on the problem of "whitewashing," see Jerome Gay, "All White Everything" in *Urban Apologetics: Restoring Black Dignity with the Gospel*, ed. Eric Mason (Grand Rapids, MI: Zondervan, 2021).

36. Hadley Hall Meares, "The Icon and the Outcast: Hattie McDaniel's Epic Double Life," *Vanity Fair*, April 26, 2021, https://www.vanityfair.com/hollywood/2021/04/hattie-mcdaniel-gone-with-the-wind-oscars-autobiography.

37. Joseph Mankiewicz, "Sidney Poitier's Trailblazing Journey to Hollywood," *Wall Street Journal*, January 15, 2022, https://www.wsj.com/articles/sidney-poitiers-trailblazing-journey-to-hollywood-11642222862.

38. For example, Philip Jenkins, *The New Face of World Christianity: Believing the Bible in the Global South* (New York: Oxford University Press, 2008).

39. On biblical interpretation, see Gordon D. Fee and Douglas Stuart, *How to Read the Bible for All It's Worth*, 4th ed. (Grand Rapids, MI: Zondervan Academic, 2014).

40. Howard Thurman, *Deep River and the Negro Spiritual Speaks of Life and Death* (Richmond, IN: Friend's Press, 1975); James Cone, *The Spirituals and the Blues*, rev. ed. (Maryknoll, NY: Orbis, 1992). Despite Cone's insights, I disagree with his black liberation theology.

41. See Jemar Tisby, *The Color of Compromise: The Truth About the American Church's Complicity in Racism* (Grand Rapids, MI: Zondervan, 2019). I disagree with some of the author's views and recommendations.

42. *Africa Bible Commentary*, ed. Tokunboh Adeyemo (Grand Rapids, MI: Zondervan Academic, 2010).

43. Esau McCaulley, "The South's Got Somethin' to Say" in *Reading While Black: African American Biblical Interpretation as an Exercise of Hope* (Downers Grove, IL: IVP Academic, 2020).

44. McCaulley, "Freedom Is No Fear" in *Reading While Black*.

45. Cone's overall method is theologically liberal and adversely affected by Marxist views of economics. It was Cone who introduced the toxic idea that Christians can use Marxist economics as an "analytical tool" for social critique. See Joe Carter, "James Cone and the Marxist Roots of Black Liberation Theology," Acton Institute Powerblog, April 30, 2018, https://

blog.acton.org/archives/101383-james-cone-and-the-marxist-roots-of-bla
ck-liberation-theology.html.

46. For how the Bible relates to the multi-ethnic urban setting, see Christopher W. Brooks, *Urban Apologetics: Answering Challenges to Faith for Urban Believers* (Grand Rapids, MI: Kregel, 2014). Brooks is a black urban pastor.

47. Glenn Loury, *One by One from the Inside Out: Essays and Reviews on Race and Responsibility in America* (New York: Free Press, 1995), 7–8.

Chapter Eight: A Christian Framework

1. Douglas Groothuis, *Christian Apologetics: A Comprehensive Case for Biblical Faith*, 2nd ed. (Downers Grove, IL: InterVarsity Press, 2022).

2. See Douglas Groothuis, *Truth Decay* (Downers Grove, IL: InterVarsity Press, 2000). See the section "Today's Modernism Against Postmodernism."

3. Steven Pinker, *How the Mind Works* (New York: W. W. Norton, 1997), 305.

4. C. S. Lewis, *Mere Christianity* (New York: HarperCollins, [1952] 2009), 8, Kindle.

5. C. S. Lewis, *The Abolition of Man* (New York: HarperOne, [1943] 2009), 33, Kindle.

6. Arthur Allen Leff, "Unnatural Ethics, Unspeakable Law," *Duke Law Review* 1979, no. 6 (December 1979), https://scholarship.law.duke.edu/cgi/viewcontent.cgi?article=2724&context=dlj.

7. References to "Enlightenment values" tend to be vague. This usually means the affirmation of reason, science, and individual rights. See Steven Pinker, *Enlightenment Now* (New York: Viking, 2018).

8. See Groothuis, "Truth Defined and Defended" in *Christian Apologetics*.

9. For a developed treatment of knowledge, see J. P. Moreland and William Lane Craig, "Knowledge and Rationality" in *Philosophical Foundations for a Christian Worldview*, 2nd ed. (Downers Grove, IL: IVP Academic, 2017).

10. Carl F. H. Henry, *God, Revelation and Authority* (Wheaton, IL: Crossway) loc. 28754–57, Kindle.

11. Francis A. Schaeffer, *He Is There and He Is Not Silent,* 30th Anniversary ed. (Carol Stream, IL: Tyndale House Publishers, [1972] 2001).

12. Stephen C. Meyer, *Return of the God Hypothesis* (New York: HarperOne, 2021).

13. Ibid., 139.

14. The Koran speaks of the first humans sinning against Allah, but they are restored shortly after. Islam has no sense of original sin as incapacitating humans from earning salvation. See Trevor Castor, "Sin According to Islam," Zwemer Center, https://www.zwemercenter.com/guide/sin-accor ding-to-muslims.

15. G. K. Chesterton, *Orthodoxy* (Sanage Publishing, [1908] 2021), 14.

16. Blaise Pascal, *Pensées* (London: Penguin Books, [1670] 2003), 36, Kindle.

17. G. K. Chesterton, *The G. K. Chesterton Collection* (Catholic Way Publishing, [1905] 2014), 109, Kindle.

18. Pascal, *Pensées*, 46.

19. Ibid., 29.

20. Robert Louis Wilken, *Liberty in the Things of God* (New Haven, CT: Yale University Press, 2019), 10, Kindle

21. Wilken, *Liberty in the Things of God*, 11, Kindle.

22. Ibid., 20.

23. See F. F. Bruce, *The Defense of the Gospel in the New Testament* (Grand Rapids, MI: Eerdmans, 1959).

24. On the mixed history of the church, see John Dickson, *Bullies and Saints* (Grand Rapids, MI: Zondervan, 2021).

25. Francis A. Schaeffer and C. Everett Koop, *Whatever Happened to the Human Race?* (Wheaton, IL: Crossway, [1979] 2021), 182–185, Kindle.

26. "Universal Declaration of Human Rights," United Nations, https://www .un.org/en/about-us/universal-declaration-of-human-rights.

27. Yuval Noah Harari, *Sapiens: A Brief History of Humankind* (New York: HarperCollins, 2015).

28. Augustine, *City of God* (London: Penguin Books, 2003), 593, Kindle.

29. Pascal, *Pensées*, 215.

30. CRT is not as utopian as classical Marxism, since it typically takes racism to be systemic and permanent. However, it seeks to overcome original sin through ineffective and counterproductive means, given its false worldview.

Chapter Nine: Fanning Holy Flames

1. Francis A. Schaeffer, *How Should We Then Live?*, L'Abri 50th Anniversary ed. (Wheaton, IL: Crossway, [1979] 2005), loc. 244–48, Kindle.

2. C. S. Lewis, *Mere Christianity* (New York: HarperCollins, [1952] 2009), 23, Kindle.

3. See J. I. Packer, *Affirming the Apostles' Creed* (Wheaton, IL: Crossway Books, 2008).

4. Francis A. Schaeffer, *Art and the Bible* (Downers Grove, IL: InterVarsity Press, [1973] 2009), 16, Kindle. See also Francis Schaeffer, *True Spirituality* (Wheaton, IL: Crossway Books, 2001).

5. Abraham Kuyper, quoted in James D. Bratt, *Abraham Kuyper: A Centennial Reader* (Grand Rapids, MI: Eerdmans, 1998), 488. For a fine introduction to Kuyper's thought and its contemporary application, see Richard Mouw, *Abraham Kuyper: A Short and Personal Introduction* (Grand Rapids, MI: Eerdmans, 2011).

6. Francis A. Schaeffer, *The God Who Is There* (Downers Grove, IL: InterVarsity Press, [1968] 2010), 174, Kindle.

7. Quoted in Os Guinness, *Time for Truth: Living Free in a World of Lies, Hype, and Spin* (Downers Grove, IL: InterVarsity Press, 2000), 44.

8. Blaise Pascal, *Pensées* (London: Penguin Books, [1670] 2003), 229, Kindle.

9. "Gaslighting" is a term in common use recently to refer to manipulation, especially in politics. The Oxford online dictionary defines this verb as: "To manipulate (a person) by psychological means into questioning his or her own sanity," https://www.oed.com/view/Entry/255554?.

10. Os Guinness, *The Magna Carta of Humanity* (Downers Grove, IL: InterVarsity Press, 2021).

11. Ibid.

12. Tocqueville, a young French aristocrat, authored the revered four-volume study called *Democracy in America* (1835-1840).

13. I recommend all of Os Guinness's books, but particularly pertinent to the American Creed, America, and its possibilities, see *The American Hour* (New York: Free Press, 1992); *A Free People's Suicide* (Downers Grove, IL: InterVarsity Press, 2012); *Last Call for Liberty* (Downers Grove, IL: InterVarsity Press, 2018); and *The Magna Carta of Humanity* (Downers Grove, IL: InterVarsity Press, 2021).

14. James Davidson Hunter, *Culture Wars: The Struggle to Define America* (New York: Basic Books, 1991). He followed this with *Before the Shooting Begins: Searching for Democracy in America's Culture Wars* (New York: Free Press, [1994] 2007).

15. John Senior, *The Death of Christian Culture* (New York: Arlington House, 1978), 54.

16. See Arthur Brooks, *Love Your Enemies: How Decent People Can Save America from the Culture of Contempt* (New York: Broadside Books,

2019). See also Os Guinness, *A Case for Civility: And Why Our Future Depends on It* (New York: HarperOne, 2008).

17. Os Guinness, *The Dust of Death* (Downers Grove, IL: InterVarsity Press), 316, Kindle. Guinness's advice on Christian activism from 1973 is pertinent today. See the entire chapter "The Third Race."

18. Shortly before his death in 1968, Malcolm X renounced his hatred of white people, left the Nation of Islam, founded a mosque, and was soon after assassinated by members of the Nation of Islam, at the urging of Louis Farrakhan, who is now the head of the Nation of Islam. See "Louis Farrakhan" at Southern Poverty Law Center: https://www.splcenter.org/fi ghting-hate/extremist-files/individual/louis-farrakhan.

19. Martin Luther King Jr., *Strength to Love* (Minneapolis, MN: Fortress Press, 2010).

20. Martin Luther King Jr., "Letter from Birmingham Jail," https://www.csu chico.edu/iege/_assets/documents/susi-letter-from-birmingham-jail.pdf.

21. It can be heard at National Public Radio: https://www.npr.org/2010/01/18 /122701268/i-have-a-dream-speech-in-its-entirety.

22. John Lewis with Kabir Sehgal, "On Good Trouble" in *Carry On: Reflections for a New Generation* (New York: Grand Central Publishing, 2021).

23. See his May 30, 2020, MSNBC interview: https://www.msnbc.com/msn bc/watch/rep-john-lewis-calls-for-peaceful-protests-as-outrage-over-geor ge-floyd-s-death-grows-84136005651. He articulates his positive, peaceful vision in a June 4, 2020, interview on CBS: https://www.cbsnews.com/vid eo/rep-john-lewis-message-to-protesters-fighting-for-racial-equality.

24. Lewis, *Carry On*, 28–30.

25. John McWhorter thinks that those totally committed to CRT will refuse any rational dialogue, so he gives strategies for not being intimidated by them. See "How Do We Work Around Them?" in *Woke Racism* (New York: Penguin, 2021).

26. Os Guinness, *Last Call for Liberty* (Downers Grove, IL: InterVarsity Press, 2018), 1, Kindle.

27. The American Presidency Project, https://www.presidency.ucsb.edu/docu ments/proclamation-97-appointing-day-national-humiliation-fasting-and -prayer. Thanks to Jim Beblavi for telling me about this.

28. Neuhaus wrote three books specifically about America, *Time Toward Home: The American Experiment as Revelation* (New York: Seabury Press, 1975); *America Against Itself: Moral Vision and Public Order* (Notre

Dame, IN: University of Notre Dame Press, 1992); and *American Babylon: Notes of a Christian Exile* (New York: Basic Books, 2009). Note the progressively pessimistic titles.

29. The *Thomas Jefferson Encyclopedia* claims this is "a spurious quotation," "although it is a generally accurate paraphrase of Jefferson's views on education," https://www.monticello.org/site/research-and-collections/edu cated-citizenry-vital-requisite-our-survival-free-people-spurious.

30. Ronald Reagan, "Farewell Address to the Nation," January 11, 1989.

31. Victor Davis Hanson, *The Dying Citizen: How Progressive Elites, Tribalism, and Globalization Are Destroying the Idea of America* (New York: Basic Books, 2021). See also Victor Davis Hanson, "The Dying Citizen: How Progressive Elites, Tribalism, and Globalization are Destroying the Idea of America," *Centennial Review* 13, no. 5 (September 2021).

32. See Os Guinness, *The Magna Carta of Humanity* (Downers Grove, IL: InterVarsity Press, 2021).

33. Personal email communication, October 5, 2021.

34. "The Oath of Allegiance," U.S. Citizenship and Immigration Services, https://www.uscis.gov/sites/default/files/document/n-400-topic-exercises /The-Oath-Of-Allegiance.pdf.

35. R. J. Rushdoony, *The Messianic Character of American Education* (Vallecito, CA: Ross House Books, 1995); Samuel Blumenfeld, *Is Public Education Necessary?* (New York: Devin-Adair Publishers, 1987).

36. Nikole Hannah-Jones, *Meet the Press*, NBC News, December 26, 2021, https://www.nbcnews.com/news/amp/ncna1286601.

37. State schools are prohibited by the First Amendment's "no establishment" clause from promoting any one religion, and that is right. However, Christians and others with set religious views need to realize the secular— and increasingly irreligious and immoral—nature of the education taught in state schools.

38. On microschools, see "About Microschools," Microschool Revolution, https://www.microschoolrevolution.com/about-microschools.

39. Philip Hamburger has made a strong, if novel, case that requiring parents to pay for state education is unconstitutional, since it requires them to support speech with which they disagree. See "Is the Public School System Constitutional?" *Wall Street Journal*, October 22, 2021, https://www.wsj .com/articles/public-school-system-constitutional-private-mcauliffe-free-sp eech-11634928722?mod=hp_trending_now_opn_pos4.

40. Thomas Sowell, *Charter Schools and Their Enemies* (New York: Basic Books, 2020).

41. My son-in-law, Christian Eidem, works in such a school—John Adams Charter School.

42. Consider this helpful resource, "Woke Schooling: A Toolkit for Concerned Parents," Manhattan Institute, June 17, 2021, https://www.manhattan-in stitute.org/woke-schooling-toolkit-for-concerned-parents.

43. Critical Race Training in Education, https://criticalrace.org.

44. Phillip W. Magness, "School Choice's Antiracist History: Vouchers Sped up Integration, While Teachers Unions Fought Them to Preserve Segregation," *Wall Street Journal*, October 18, 2021, https://www.wsj.com /articles/school-choice-antiracist-history-integration-funding-segregation -11634568700.

45. Ibid. Friedman was an influential Jewish free-market economist.

46. It is never too early to teach apologetics to young people. Consider the ministry of Mama Bear Apologetics (mamabearapologetics.com) for younger children and Summit Ministries (summit.org) for junior high and high school students.

47. Voddie Baucham, *Fault Lines: The Social Justice Movement and Evangelicism's Looming Catastrophe* (Washington, D.C.: Salem Books, 2021).

48. Owen Strachan, *Christianity and Wokeness: How the Social Justice Movement Is Hijacking the Gospel—and the Way to Stop It* (Washington, D.C.: Salem Books, 2021).

49. See Dru Johnson, *Human Rites: The Power of Rituals, Habits, and Sacraments* (Grand Rapids, MI: Eerdmans, 2019).

50. Guinness, *The Magna Carta of Humanity*, 245.

51. See the information at Daughters of the American Revolution, https://www .dar.org/national-society/education/constitution-week.

52. Hillsdale College offers an excellent, free online course on the Constitution: "The Meaning and History of the Constitution," https://online.hillsdale .edu/landing/constitution-101. I also highly recommend this school for a college education along with Colorado Christian University, which also upholds traditional American values.

53. U. S. Constitution Week, Grand Lake, Colorado, https://www.grandlake usconstitutionweek.com.

54. Alexis Carr, "Black Americans Who Served in WWII Faced Segregation at Home and Abroad," History.com, August 5, 2020, https://www.history.com/news/black-soldiers-world-war-ii-discrimination.

55. Annie Karni and Luke Broadwater, "Biden Signs Law Making Juneteenth a National Holiday," *New York Times*, June 17, 2021, https://www.nytimes.com/2021/06/17/us/politics/juneteenth-holiday-biden.html.

56. See African American History Month, https://www.africanamericanhistorymonth.gov.

57. See also Mike Gonzalez, *BLM: The Making of a New Marxist Revolution* (New York: Encounter Books, 2021).

58. 4 U.S. Code § 4–Pledge of allegiance to the flag; manner of delivery, https://www.law.cornell.edu/uscode/text/4/4.

59. Robert H. Bork, *Slouching Towards Gomorrah* (New York: HarperCollins ebooks, 2010), 148, Kindle. Bork was an esteemed law professor and judge who was nominated by Ronald Reagan for a seat on the Supreme Court in 1987. Sadly, he was not confirmed. *Slouching Towards Gomorrah* presages much of what is wrong with America today and overlaps with much of what I have written in this book.